OF A BOY AND HIS VALLEY

Of A Boy And His Valley

Life in rural Western New York

during the Great Depression 1929-1936

by

Arnold W. Cook

Illustrations by Sylvia Sprowl Duttweiler

Windswept Press
Interlaken, New York
1991

Re-Order From
Arnold W. Cook
20831 Frank Waters Rd.
Stanwood, WA 98292

SECOND PRINTING 1993

ABC Nature Reflections

ISBN: 1-55787-082-9

Printed in the
United States of America

A quality publication by

Heart of the Lakes Publishing
Interlaken, New York 14847

DEDICATED TO THE MEMORY OF

Donald A. Sprowl

A true and loyal friend
who shared with me many of the experiences
related in this account

ACKNOWLEDGMENTS

I gratefully acknowledge the enthusiastic assistance of many people in sharing with me their recollections of the events recorded in this book, especially May Sprowl Ruhl, Ethel Glow Lee, Lillian Woodard Bowen, Preston Steinbar, Minnie Reed Beach, and Katherine Lincoln Macdonald, my teacher during those Depression years. Of special help in researching some of the detail was Kenneth Kysor, Cattaraugus County Historian. Evelyn Bence provided valuable suggestions on style. Of special note is Sylvia Sprowl Duttweiler, daughter of Donald Sprowl, who not only penned the original ink drawings, but who also spent many hours typesetting the manuscript for publication. From the inception of this project to completion, I have appreciated the constructive suggestions and encouragement of my wife, Betty.

Table of Contents

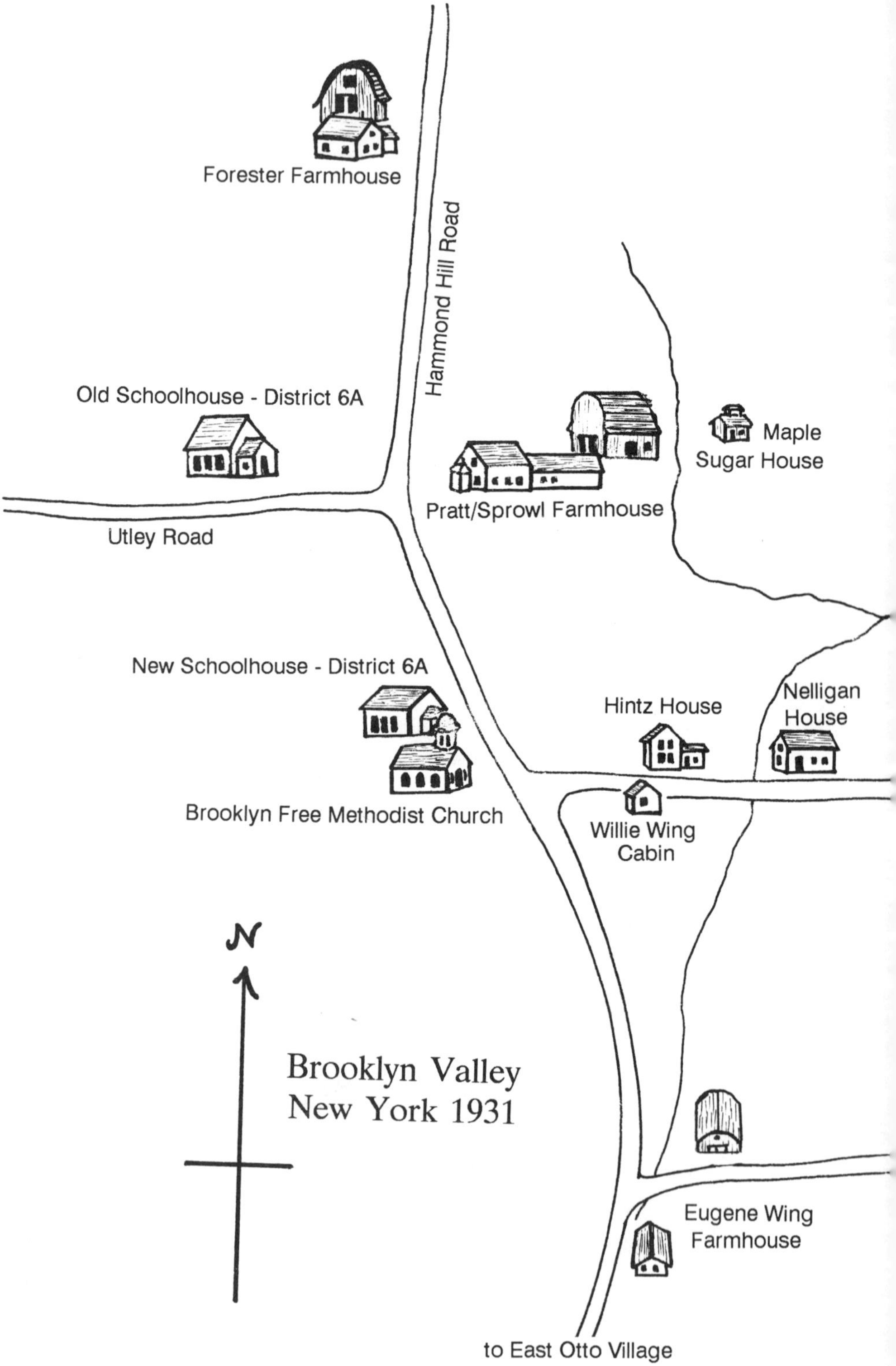
Forester Farmhouse
Hammond Hill Road
Old Schoolhouse - District 6A
Maple
Sugar House
Pratt/Sprowl Farmhouse
Utley Road
New Schoolhouse - District 6A
Nelligan
House
Hintz House
Brooklyn Free Methodist Church
Willie Wing
Cabin
N
Brooklyn Valley
New York 1931
Eugene Wing
Farmhouse
to East Otto Village

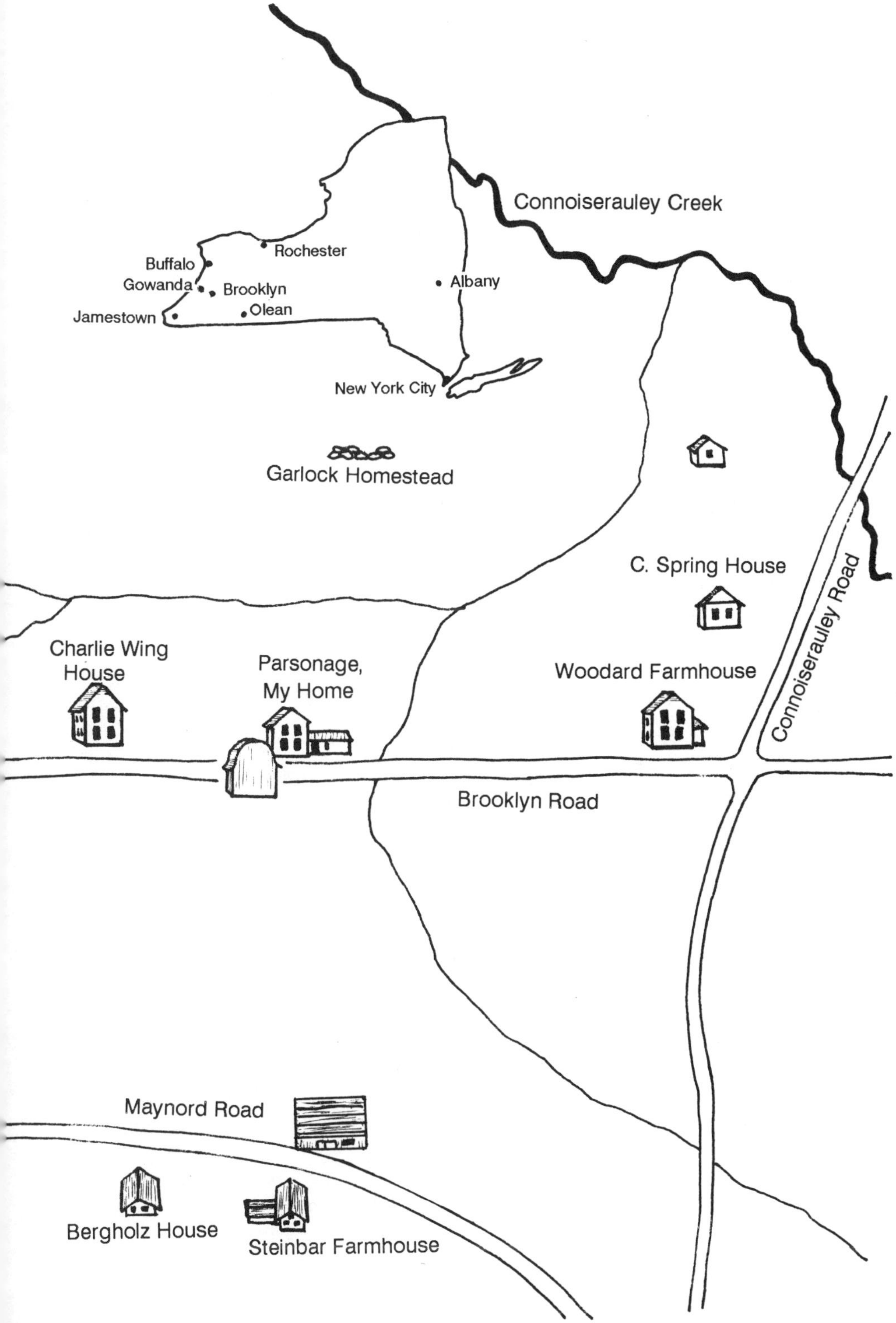

Connoiserauley Creek
Rochester
Buffalo
Gowanda
Brooklyn
Albany
Jamestown
Olean
New York City
Garlock Homestead
C. Spring House
Connoiserauley Road
Charlie Wing House
Parsonage, My Home
Woodard Farmhouse
Brooklyn Road
Maynord Road
Bergholz House
Steinbar Farmhouse

"He'll Never Walk"

"Look, Betty, from up here we can see the entire valley!" I pointed off to the west. "There's the church. That white structure next to it was the schoolhouse. See the parsonage and barn beside the big elm. And off to the east Mock Hill stands guard." Eagerly I introduced my red-haired wife to the landmarks of Brooklyn Valley. I wanted to share with her this chapter of my life.

"Why are there apple trees way up here in this pasture?" Betty queried. "I don't see a house near here."

"Look at those foundation stones over there," I pointed. "This is the old Garlock farm. The buildings were all gone even when I first climbed this hill as a little boy."

"That must seem like a long time ago," Betty mused. "Seeing it again probably brings back memories."

* * * * *

"He'll never walk. But I think he has a good mind," the old

country doctor spoke kindly but honestly to my parents. Dr. Williams had just assisted at my arrival into the world on a cold and miserable 29th of March in 1922. Both of my misshapen feet were grotesquely twisted and turned backwards. The place of my birth was the white frame Free Methodist parsonage nestled in a tiny settlement bearing the name of Brooklyn.

Several conflicting stories explained the origin of such a pretentious name for so tiny a community. By one account, the locals jokingly referred to the span over the modest stream flowing past the cheese factory as "Brooklyn Bridge." This appellation later expanded to the nearby area.

Another explanation involved the little Free Methodist Church erected at the T of the crossroads in 1870. A famous church trial raged in the New York City borough of Brooklyn at the same time that a difference of opinion surfaced in the small congregation at the crossroads. In jest, someone drew the comparison with the city church in New York City. Whatever its origin, the name has adhered for over a century.

The small valley, tied so closely to my childhood, spread between hills forested with sugar maple, beech, ash, basswood, oak, cherry, ironwood, and hemlock. Small dairy farms constituted the only economic activity of consequence for those living in the valley. The nearest village, East Otto, lay three miles to the south of the valley and acted as the center of trade for the area.

Aside from its uniqueness to me as the only place of my birth, this cluster of small farms offered little to distinguish it from countless other rural communities across America. My father, the Rev. Elmer J. Cook, and his wife, Eva, had come to Brooklyn on his first appointment as a pastor in the Genesee Conference a year and a half before my birth.

In that era, pastors of Free Methodist Churches were moved to new appointments on the average of every two years. It was reputed that when my father pulled into the parsonage yard upon return from annual conference, the chickens would lie down on their backs to have their feet tied for moving to the next place.

After three years at Brooklyn, our family moved to Belfast, a small village along the Genesee River in Allegany County. My only brother, Irving, arrived during father's two-year stay at Belfast. Our next move was to Cattaraugus, the village which bore the name of the county.

Somewhat softened by memory are the painful recollections of attempts to improve the condition of my feet. During the first year of my life came the operations at the Mountain Clinic in Olean where my feet were broken and forced to face forward. Next I suffered through a series of casts up to each knee, forcing my feet into the desired configurations. A woman doctor carried out this procedure in Utica. The moment the old casts came off, new ones tightly encased my feet and legs with their stern grip. I always pleaded for a respite between casts - but in vain.

When the casts finally came off for good, the doctor prescribed placing my feet in icy water for ten minutes both morning and night to stimulate circulation. It usually required father and mother to restrain me and keep the feet under water. After releasing my feet from the icy bath, my parents rubbed them briskly with a coarse towel until the skin showed pink and my toes tingled.

Steel braces from my feet to my waist felt like shackles during waking hours. Finally, a shoemaker in Utica built successive pairs of corrective shoes for me. Each pair became distorted and scuffed as my feet grew. These cost $25.00 a pair when ordinary shoes sold for $1.49. Now I marvel at the sacrifices my parents made to help me walk. Although not like normal boys, walk I did, but with a peculiar gait.

The year 1929 was memorable for two reasons: the stock market crash ushering in the Great Depression and my father's acceptance of the assignment to return to the church in Brooklyn. No one else was willing to go to this circuit, the least-desirable in the entire Genesee Conference. At six years of age, I made the twelve-mile move with my family from Cattaraugus back to the house where I was born. Experiences of the next seven Depression years as a boy in Brooklyn Valley, exerted a profound influence on my view of life.

Fiery Nightmare

"Is breakfast almost ready?" I asked Mother for the fifth time as I paced impatiently from living room to kitchen. The night before I had scarcely slept as thoughts of the new school raced through my head. I checked my pencil box, tablet, drinking cup, and lunch box again to make certain I had everything I would need.

Regular school attendance was always important to me as I was growing up. I disliked missing classes and avoided being late. One problem arose by my being part of a Free Methodist parsonage family. The annual conference, at which assignment of pastors was made for the following year, occurred Labor Day weekend. Until appointments were read by the Bishop as almost the last action of the business sessions, often late Saturday night, I was unsure where I would be going to school for the next year.

Once father returned home, moving even our meager furnishings required a little time to pack and arrange for one of the farmers to haul them in his open truck. The result usually was my starting a day or more after classes had begun. Being very self-conscious about my feet, I felt conspicuous arriving after the other students had already settled in. Drawing attention to myself was what I wished to avoid. But this was one of the burdens I had to bear as a PK.

On my first day at East Otto District No. 6A, my father chauffeured me to school in the 1928 Chevy and delivered me to the classroom veteran, Mrs. Wing, for whom this was the last year of teaching before retirement. Looking down at me from what seemed like a great distance, she asked the question: "Young man, what grade are you to be in?"

Since I had completed kindergarten and first grade at Cattaraugus, I replied: "Second grade."

Looking thoughtful, she paused for what seemed a very long time before making the pronouncement: "No. There aren't any other students in second grade this year. You will be in third grade."

The speed of this promotion dazzled me. And to this day I'm not really certain what I missed by not taking second grade. Since this one-room school usually offered all eight grades, I'm sure that Mrs. Wing looked forward to the omission of one eighth of the classes through this logical solution.

The schoolhouse for District No. 6A, located on Utley Road near its intersection with Hammond Hill Road, was a plain-looking white clapboarded structure consisting of one main room plus a small entryway or cloakroom for hanging wraps and stowing boots and lunches. Adjacent to the entryway were the two restrooms of the type involving no plumbing. The teacher granted permission to use these facilities as a student raised the appropriate number of fingers. Several sugar maple trees provided shade and softened the starkness of the setting. Adjacent to one side of the school yard, just beyond the perimeter of its board fence, lay a small cemetery used by a few local families.

A wood-fired furnace standing in the right front corner of the room provided heat. In partial payment of his school taxes, a local farmer provided the wood supply to satisfy its enormous appetite. During noon hours, two or three of the older boys split the big logs with double-bitted axes. One of the teacher's many responsibilities was to stoke the furnace. Cantankerously independent, the heater offered two levels of heat: "Too cold" and "too hot."

All of the water for drinking or other purposes had to be carried in pails by the larger boys from the outdoor pump at the Pratt farm, a few hundred feet away. What didn't slosh away in transit was poured into a covered cylindrical container with a spigot. Each student was supposed to supply a cup for personal use. The standard model, costing ten cents, was an ingenious device. Composed of four or five tapered metal bands of progressive diameter and a solid bottom section, it could be pulled out and twisted slightly to lock it into drinking cup shape. Then it could be collapsed for storage in the desk. Easily bent out of shape, often cups would leak. The sterility of these folding cups was indeed questionable. It was not unusual for the cup to collapse while in use, drenching the unwary pupil.

The desk and bench units were constructed of a cast iron frame painted black with wooden desk tops and seats. The seat for one unit was attached to the same frame as the desk for the one behind it. These units were screwed to the floor in rows. Separating individual students by moving desks was an impossibility. As a consequence, the person sitting behind you always had golden opportunities to make life miserable in ingenious ways. Girls with their hair in pigtails were easy victims to having them "fall" into the inkwell of the person behind them.

One day in the fall of my second year at this school is forever etched sharply in memory. The morning of November 26, 1930, began in a normal fashion. I walked the three-quarters of a mile from the parsonage to school, hurrying to get there on time. Because father often prayed for many concerns at family devotions after breakfast, the margin of time in which to reach school punctually was often slim. My attempts to buffer this time period by advancing the hands on the Elgin clock in the living room by ten or fifteen minutes were short-lived after father's discovery of my ploy.

I had just trudged into the school yard, damp and cold from the wind which had been hurling a mixture of wet snow and rain in my face, as the teacher appeared at the door ringing the hand bell to signal the end of play and the beginning of classes. The morning droned away as she called up each class, starting with the lowest grades and proceeding up the ranks. The noon hour passed quickly as students played games at the board or read, since the weather was too unpleasant for outside activities.

The teacher, Miss Edith Wehling, had several times replenished the wood in the furnace. The room seemed unusually hot, almost stifling. At two o'clock in the afternoon, one class was at the front of the room reciting. Almost simultaneously I saw flames start licking through the wall at the front of the room and sensed the acrid irritation of smoke in my nose and throat. The fire had made fast headway between the inside and outside walls before breaking through into the room around the stovepipe.

"Fire! Fire! Get outside," the teacher ordered. She dispatched one of the older boys to run to the Pratt farmhouse where there was a phone. Already the sight of the smoke and blaze had brought neighbors running or driving to the fire. The pitifully meager supply of water in the container, usually not over five gallons at peak and approaching empty near the close of the school day, was hardly a token. Some farmers tried desperately to carry water from the pump at Pratts in pails or milk cans. Others yanked some of the seats loose from the floor and carried them out along with the globe and library books. The teacher rounded up the students and kept them at a safe distance. The futile efforts to save the building ceased as flames totally engulfed the structure. That school day ended early!

But for me that was far from the end of its frightening effects. Many nights afterwards I awoke in terror as the flames were a constant element in nightmares which left me in a cold sweat, fearing to return to sleep lest the flaming vision repeat itself.

Two years after the new school building had been occupied, a second occasion threatened to repeat the fiery consequences. As far as water source, nothing had changed since the old schoolhouse except that the new one was built near the church. Again, in the middle of recitations, we smelled smoke and saw flames around the stovepipe. Leaving the older boys to cope there, I raced the several hundred feet to the Pratt farmhouse to give the alarm and get a fire extinguisher. Finding no one there except Grandma Pratt, I grabbed the big extinguisher and carried it to the school only to discover that the fire was out. When I later attempted to pick up the extinguisher, I could scarcely lift it. The adrenaline had reduced its flow and only normal strength remained. Little damage was done and school was not dismissed even for one day.

The specter of fire in that little farming community was ever-present, as no effective means of fire protection was available. With electricity unavailable, the kerosene lanterns in the barn and kerosene lamps for house illumination added to the hazards presented by heating with wood stoves. Hay stored too green was another prime cause of barn fires. I can't remember a single instance where a fire was extinguished once it really got started. Lack of adequate water sources doomed the valiant efforts made to save buildings. Neighbors and friends would rush to the scene and attempt to turn livestock loose if it was a barn or salvage household effects from a home. Throwing items of furniture from a second story window often destroyed them as effectively as had they been left to burn.

One particularly sad case occurred when the Bergholtz farmhouse and barn on top of Hammond Hill burned on September 26, 1934. Banks had failed and people were reluctant to trust their money to their custody. Mary Bergholtz had, over time, secreted their savings to make payment on the farm mortgage. The accumulation of currency was stored behind a loose brick in the chimney. I recall with great clarity her grief as her hoard of paper money was discovered reduced to ashes. Consequently she gave up the farm. These were difficult days in our valley.

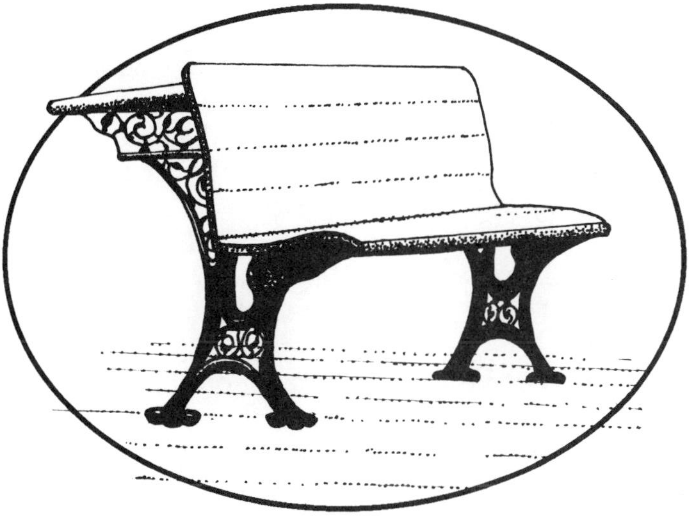

Strange Semester

After the old schoolhouse burned in early winter, finding a temporary place to hold classes presented a real problem. The community was small, so options available were few. Some people thought this an auspicious time to merge with East Otto Union School in the village three miles away. However, enough voters wished to retain the district school so their will prevailed. After several school board meetings presided over by chairman Frank Woodard, the location for interim classes was selected and the site for the new building chosen.

The location decided on for temporary classroom space should have delighted me. It was right next door to the parsonage in a house owned by Charles Wing. Some years before, the two rooms facing the road had housed a small grocery store. These were now vacant as Mr. Wing lived in the back portion of the building. Of all of the pupils in the district, I now lived nearest the school.

The old desks, salvaged during the fire, were installed in one room and faced a newly-purchased blackboard. The other room was used for storing wraps, lunches, and what remained of the library. Most of the library books had been saved, although a majority of the volumes were old and would not have been much of a loss. Soon classes were convened in these rather unusual facilities.

From my point of view, I soon discovered the change to be not entirely favorable. The fact that I could reach the school in only three minutes prompted my parents to decide that I should come home for lunch. Not having to prepare lunches freed up time for my mother around breakfast and other farm activities. Chores and other duties soon multiplied to keep me occupied at home during the noon hour. Consequently I missed participating in the major play period of the day.

Secondly, I became aware that most of what went on around the outside of the school building was within easy view of the parsonage. It wasn't that I was doing things of which they would disapprove. Simply, I didn't like to be so visible. I disliked having to explain to my parents some of the happenings they had observed. A seasoned teacher might have found better ways to handle problems caused by this deficient school environment. Still, the physical setting contributed significantly to the disruptions.

Christmas vacation was reduced to only the holiday itself to make up the days lost during the transition to the new premises after the school burned. Christmas exercises were entirely omitted. The students resented missing out on this high point in the school year. The restive attitude of the pupils reflected their frustration and disappointment at forfeiting the normal holiday season.

The coming of spring brought not only maple sugar season but also an epidemic of spring fever. The sun shone into that small room crowded with farm children whose norm was one bath a week on Saturday night. Footwear worn to the dairy barn carried more than the odor of leather and rubber. It is easy to see why on warm May and June afternoons Miss Wehling surrendered to student requests that we sit on the grassy ditch bank beside the road for study hour. Under these conditions, even a great disciplinarian would have been challenged to capture and hold the attention of children from ages five to fifteen years. Every vehicle which went past, every cardinal and rose-breasted grosbeak serenading in the huge sugar maples across the road, every bark of a dog across the valley, and a variety of lively insects tasting portions of the pupils' anatomy afforded distractions from arithmetic, reading, and writing.

In the pasture behind the school flowed a small creek which was just the right size to dam up at a deep point to produce a swimming hole. Some of the students inveigled the teacher to join them by the creek to eat lunch. Alas, my parents refused to let me take part in their fun. As time went on, the moment of return to resume the afternoon session began to extend beyond one o'clock. On at least one occasion their return to class came after the hour of two. My parents insisted that I wait on our porch until the group returned. I was frustrated in my efforts to devise a way to take part in this relaxed lunchtime. These and other activities became the source of questions by not only my parents but also the parents of other students.

In mid-April the teacher announced a unit on nature study for the fourth and fifth grades.

"I want each of you to bring to school on Friday an object from the out-of-doors to place in a nature exhibit," Miss Wehling explained. "Don't forget."

I looked at Don Sprowl and he winked back. After school we headed for the creek. From the alders along the stream we cut forked sticks. Near the end of one of these we attached a loop of string with a staple to guide it. Under Brooklyn Bridge below the barn we found what we sought - a good-sized water snake.

Don pinned it down with his forked stick. I slid the loop of string over its head. The snake thrashed vigorously at the end of my stick. It didn't want to go to school and gave us quite a tussle before we were able to deposit it in a wooden box which we had prepared. Placing heavy screen over the top, we slipped a frog into the box for its supper.

"I can't wait until the teacher sees our specimen," Don grinned as he jumped on his bike to peddle home.

The next morning we were eager to be the first to display our nature specimen. Poor Miss Wehling almost fainted when we raised the lid. We narrowly prevented the snake's escape from the box.

"Take that away at once,' the teacher ordered. "Snakes do not belong in the classroom."

"We were just trying to do what you asked us to," we explained, pleading our innocence and good faith. The teacher was totally unimpressed.

Shortly after the snake episode, I became ill with a fever which lasted three or four days and caused me to miss classes. I awoke one morning feeling just fine. I got dressed for school and was about to leave the house.

"Let me look at you," mother demanded. After brief scrutiny, she reached her conclusion.

"You have measles. Get right back to bed."

Mine were the nine day variety and caused me to miss a total of two weeks of school. In addition, the health officer appeared to quarantine the house. He fastened a large red sign to the front door to warn people to stay away.

Isolation had happened before in Cattaraugus when my brother, Irving, had a severe case of scarlet fever. Then even father couldn't go away from the premises. He placed a list of grocery needs in the oven along with money to pay for them. These were heated until hopefully any germs were killed. A neighbor took the list and money from the porch and brought back the needed supplies. Being sick was no fun in those days.

The sound of a car driving into the school yard in mid-morning alerted the students to a possible diversion from the daily routine. Whispered guesses circulated in the room.

"I was right this time," I whispered to Lillian as the teacher opened the door to welcome the County Superintendent of Schools. The conversational buzz quickly subsided into an awkward hush.

Quality control of education in that era had at least two dimensions. One was the periodic visit of the County School Superintendent to each school. The man filling this post for Cattaraugus County was Mr. Levi R. Tubbs. He was a well-rounded grandfatherly gentleman as even his name implied. After consulting with the teacher, he selected students at random from each grade to recite for him. The questions he put were representative for the grade and subject. The awe with which we viewed him strongly affected our responses. Along with the rest of the students, I desperately hoped he would not call my name. Harry, Carol, and

Clair had each been called.

"Arnold Cook?" he looked inquiringly around.

"Yes sir." I arose and went forward, stumbling over Clinton's foot. A titter went around the room and my face began to burn.

"Please name the continents for me," he requested.

My voice quavered and my knees shook as I haltingly gave the correct response.

Next he tried my arithmetic skills by posing a word problem which required division. Although my answer was right, the voice in which it was given lacked conviction.

To his final query, "Do you enjoy reading books?" I finally was able to crack a smile.

"Yes sir, I really do."

The second, and more comprehensive, evaluation of the outcomes of the educational process, came in the form of standardized tests for each subject. These were prepared by the New York State Board of Regents but were administered by the teacher. The questions were printed on tissue paper and enclosed in sealed envelopes printed with the precise day and hour at which they were to be opened and distributed to the students. A certain hush always accompanied this ritual as the teacher cut the end from the envelope and passed out the questions.

The outcomes of these tests determined not only if a student would pass but also judged the teacher's effectiveness. That June the result for a number of students from District 6A was repetition of the grade. For the teacher, one consequence was failure to receive a contract for the following academic year. In the autumn of 1931, we had a new teacher and a brand new building.

The Medicine That Saved Christmas

"EAST OTTO DISTRICT 6A
TO BUILD NEW SCHOOL"

The above item appeared on the front page and rated its own heading in "The Cattaraugus Times." Usually news of our valley was buried among the personals under a caption: "Interesting News of East Otto and Vicinity."

A new schoolhouse for District 6A was exciting news in the Brooklyn community. The one which burned had been a landmark, as it had been in use for over sixty years. It was by no means the first educational structure in the locality, that distinction going to a school taught by John Pratt somewhere on Hammond Hill Road.

The New York State Education Department mandated selection of a different site for the school, citing two deficiencies of the old location. A larger area was deemed necessary for a playground. In case a well was ever drilled, having a cemetery just uphill from the school was thought inappropriate. Albert Pratt offered to donate half an acre of land if the school board would purchase a like amount from him. The spot decided upon was just north of the Free Methodist Church, reducing by four minutes my walk to school.

Action by the school board specified a cost of not over $5,000. Insurance from the burned structure amounted to $1,750. Out of eight sealed bids, the lowest totaled $2,395. Actual work on the building didn't get started until August 6, 1931. Even so, classes began there in September. New single-unit desks in a variety of sizes were a great improvement over the old combination units which had been screwed to the floor.

Our new teacher was Miss Katherine Lincoln whose home was between Brooklyn and East Otto village. Early that fall George Fleckenstein's milk truck frequently halted in front of the schoolhouse. George appeared at the door for a brief conversation with the teacher. All of the students displayed great interest in these developments.

My classmate Don nudged me. "I'll bet he's asking her for a date," he whispered.

"Why don't you ask her if he did?" I countered.

"Quiet!" Lillian interrupted. "Let's see if we can hear what they're saying.

Just then Miss Lincoln closed the door and came back into the room. Seeing our impish, inquisitive faces all turned in her direction, she blushed and tried to turn our attention back to our lessons.

"Fifth Grade Arithmetic," the teacher announced as routine took over again. Later in the day, while she was briefly absent from the room, this scrawled message appeared on the blackboard, "Teacher has a date."

Resumption of the customary Christmas festivities that December was a joyful occasion. We felt the holiday season had really begun when Don's grandfather, Albert Pratt, arrived with a wagon load of lumber with which he erected a temporary stage or platform about a foot or so high across the front of the schoolroom. He strung a wire above the stage from one side of the room to the other. Volunteers brought bed sheets from home which we hung on the wire to create stage curtains. On one disastrous occasion, in the middle of an act a supporting hook pulled out of the wall, dropping the sheets to the floor. To the consternation of the cast, they were exposed to audience view while in the middle of changing costumes.

The second sure sign of the season was the appearance of a local farmer carrying a big Christmas tree. Decorating the tree called for ingenuity, for most of the trimmings had to be improvised by the students. We pasted together paper chains of rainbow hues and created cutouts by folding long pieces of paper in various ways to form repeated figures or objects. Such activities served as our art lessons. A tasty standard feature was the stringing of garlands of popcorn. We never permitted ALL of it to reach the tree. The teacher brought a few shiny ornaments to hang on the branches along with red apples. Mothers baked and decorated molasses cookies. A loop of string baked into the top of each cookie made it easy to attach it to the limbs. The defective ones whose strings came loose dropped the cookies to the floor in a crumbly heap. We eagerly salvaged these rejects for instant taste testing. We weren't above helping to create some of these "accidents."

For two reasons we had no lights on the tree. First, electricity was not available. Second, real candles which some used sparingly at home were banned from school due to the fire hazard they created. At home we had eight or ten little tin candle holders which clipped to the branches. Each one had a socket which held a small candle three or four inches tall. Due to the cost of candles plus the fire danger, they were lit only for short periods of time under the supervision of adults who had a pail of water close at hand. At home we had one near conflagration. A dry hemlock branch caught fire. It burned furiously. Mother doused the flaming branch before major damage occurred.

The Christmas program at school was composed of a combination of individual and group recitations and songs plus a number of short plays or dramatizations. While the theme was in keeping with the season, often the mini dramas were intended to be humorous and bore titles such as "Mehitabel and Jerusha." The teacher reduced regular classes or suspended some to give time for practice. This was especially the case as the day neared for the performance. The program took place in the evening so parents and everyone in the neighborhood could attend. Invariably the schoolhouse was so packed that some people were forced to stand. To miss this annual event for any reason was considered one of the worst things that could occur to a pupil.

"Son, I don't think you're well enough to attend the Christmas program." I was stunned.

In mid-December 1931 I had been running a temperature due to the flu. At mother's stern pronouncement, my world fell apart. During the years of the Great Depression, the annual school Christmas program shone as a bright spot in that little one-room schoolhouse. Missing the only Christmas festivities of the entire year seemed more than I could handle.

I had already been psyched up in helping to decorate the tree and by daily practice of recitations, songs, and skits. With only fifteen students spread over eight grades, I, along with others, had memorized and practiced multiple parts. Besides missing participation in the program, I feared losing out on the exchange of gifts presided over by Santa Claus. Too, I didn't want to miss the distribution of the little red mesh bags of hard candy which included one chocolate. My despair deepened as I pondered this unfair fate.

After lunch, as they were leaving to visit a sick parishioner, mother and father cautioned: "Stay quietly by the stove and rest." No sooner had they departed than I had an inspiration. One of the remedies peddled by Hayden Silvernail, the Watkins dealer, was a potent brown liquid named Watkins Liniment. Directions on the bottle read: "Apply externally to aching joints and muscles. For internal use, mix a half teaspoon of liniment into a glass of warm water and drink."

Recognizing the precariousness of my situation, I wanted a miracle, even one of my own making. I reasoned that if a little of the stuff was beneficial, a greater dose would be even more effective. I poured a glass half full of the medication and finished filling it with warm water. From previous experience, I knew the potion would be bitter and burn. The only way to get it down was to swallow it quickly without stopping to breathe. Once again that technique worked.

Gasping for breath, I felt my insides aflame. Chills shook my body. In total misery, dreading my parents' return, I wrapped myself in a quilt and huddled next to the roaring wood stove.

The moment mother entered the house she exclaimed: "What do I smell?" I had been burping the horrible stuff. Since it was alcohol based, it's a wonder the fumes from my breath hadn't caught fire!

"You know how much I hate taking Watkins Liniment," I pleaded. How well mother did know that! "I wanted so much to get well enough to go to the Christmas program that I took a strong dose."

"How strong," mother demanded. She gasped when I admitted that it was a 50/50 mixture.

"Let me take your temperature," she insisted.

From the burning within, I expected the mercury to soar. Twice she returned the thermometer to my mouth before reluctantly admitting: "It reads normal."

"Then I can go!" I shouted, jumping up and down in my excitement.

Mother hesitated, and then agreed. To the concession she attached a stern proviso: "Promise me that you will never pull this stunt again."

"I promise," was my prompt reply.

That was one promise that I kept scrupulously. However, I still remember Watkins Liniment as "the medicine that saved Christmas."

Merely Child's Play

"Anti-eye over," Preston yelled as he hurled the rubber ball over the peak of the schoolhouse roof, starting one more round of our favorite outdoor game.

"Anti-eye over," the call came from the other side. Apparently they hadn't caught the ball before it reached the ground, so were now returning it over the roof. Don caught the ball which had gone high over the corner, but did touch the roof - making it a legal ball. Part of our team scurried around one corner of the building while the rest ran the opposite way. All pretended to be holding the ball, trying to fool the opposing team who scattered and tried to reach the other side of the schoolhouse. Don's aim was good. The ball hit Clinton Woodard, so he became a member of our team.

On the next round, the other side caught the ball. They came charging around so quickly that Carol and I both were hit before we could escape to safety across the line parallel with our side of the structure. On the following exchange a shouting match attempted to determine whether Harry Silvernail had been struck before or after passing the corner. In the middle of this fracas, Miss Lincoln appeared at the door ringing the hand bell to announce the beginning of classes. At recess, play resumed until all of the opposite side had been tagged and claimed by our team.

* * * * *

Preston Steinbar tossed the softball bat to Clair Woodard who grabbed it with one hand. Preston placed his hand around the bat above Clair's hold. They alternated until Preston's hand was so close to the end of the bat that Clair had insufficient space for all of his fingers. So Preston had the first choice for his team. "Harry," he yelled. Harry came to his side. Clair chose his brother, Clinton. Team members were chosen in the order of their perceived athletic ability.

"Bob." "Don." "Lillian." "Ed." "May." As the unchosen group dwindled, I braced myself for the usual humiliation. It was Clair's turn to choose and I was the only one left. "I'll take Arnold," he said without enthusiasm. As much as I wanted to play, always being left until last was painful.

Up at bat first, Clair hit a home run. Batting was in the order of our choice. When my turn came, we had two outs. I swung on the first pitch - missing it completely. On the second try, I ticked the ball. The next time my bat encountered nothing but air. "Third out," Preston called. So I went out to left field, the least likely place for action. Preston hit a fast ground ball almost directly at me. I missed it completely. He rounded third base before I reached it and pegged it to Clair. Keenly I sensed the disappointment of my team mates. My further contributions to the team continued in a similar vein. When the game ended, I was glad to escape unhappy reality by joining an intrepid African explorer through the pages of a library book.

* * * * *

I realized why I was last to be chosen. My foot problems made it impossible to run as fast as normal. When at bat, I couldn't seem to hit the ball. In the field, I missed the ball more often than I caught it. The other students seemed almost relieved when I stayed inside to read instead of joining them on the field. Then a marvelous thing happened.

"See the pheasants over in the potato field," father called. I looked, but couldn't spot them. "Right over there," he pointed. I still was unable to see them. Both father and mother had begun to notice my seeming inability to see things far away and this last episode forced them to wonder if I had a real vision problem. A week later Dr. Hanvey, a Jamestown optometrist, concluded: "He is extremely near-sighted and has astigmatism." I was vindicated.

With glasses, a whole new world opened up to me. Before, I had not realized what I was missing. To my delight, my batting record improved so dramatically that I was chosen fairly early in the selection process and one of my team members would run the bases for me. My self-esteem was given a much-needed boost.

* * * * *

Snow had fallen steadily the previous night and by Monday an undisturbed blanket a foot deep covered the acre of land on which the school stood starkly, unadorned by a single tree or shrub. As red-cheeked students straggled in from three directions, the word was passed around, "Don't mess up the snow." At noon, the reason for this admonition became clear. The conditions were perfect for a game of Fox and Geese.

Preston naturally took charge of laying out the course in the snow. He walked around in a very large circle. Then he bisected the circle with several tracks creating a figure like a wheel and spokes. "All set," he called. "I'll be the fox on this first round."

We all scattered to various positions on this figure tramped out in the powdery snow. At a signal, Preston tried to catch someone. All had to stay strictly on the designated tracks. First to be tagged was Ethel. Then Hank, and Ralph, and Douglas. The last to be caught was Harry, who then automatically was the fox for the next chase. Lots of energy was worked off in this strenuous game.

Getting bored after several rounds, Carol suggested: "Let's do Hare and Hounds." Enthusiastic approval set us to laying out an even more intricate track in the snow. This was composed of loops and turns of varied design spread out over a large area. The hare could jump across from one loop to another while the hounds had to follow the tracks. Hank started off as the hare, but soon was tagged by Don who then became the hare. Given a fair start, the chase continued. The genius of this game was that no one was forced to wait on the sidelines. All could continue to participate until the bell rang or we tired of the chase.

* * * * *

"I got a new jackknife," I confided to Dick Bergholtz.

"Let's see it," he responded.

Proudly I pulled out my treasure. At one end were two blades - a large one and a small one. This model boasted a third slim blade at the opposite end. The shiny treasure had been my only birthday present. But I was delighted, as it replaced a rather disreputable model with nicked and corroded blades.

A thaw had turned the playground into a slushy mess, practically ruining the tracks for outdoor games. It was even too nasty weather to make forts and have a snowball fight. At recess Dick challenged me to a game of mumbledy-peg. Out in the woodshed we found a pine board about a foot wide and set it up on two blocks of firewood.

"You go first," Dick offered.

With the small blade extended parallel to the handle and the large blade at a ninety-degree angle, ! grasped my knife's handle at the opposite end from the blades. With a flick of the wrist, I sent the knife revolving in the air until it came to rest on the board. "Yippee!" I yelled as the small blade stuck in the plank, the rest of the knife held aloft. That gave me 100 points.

On my next throw, the large blade entered the board with the end of the handle touching the wood. "Just 25," I conceded. My third try failed to puncture the board and the knife clattered to the ground.

Dick's first try accomplished embedding the small blade but with the large blade also touching the wood. "Seventy-five," he noted. The following flip found just the large blade embedded. "Fifty," I noted. After a hundred and another fifty, he missed the plank and it was my turn again. Reaching one thousand, he was the winner.

I remember no serious injury from all of the boy-hours devoted to this game. And it offered a potential far less serious in consequences than two or three lads with double-bitted axes splitting logs for the stove in the confines of the small woodshed at the rear of the building. I can imagine the liability insurance costs as well as concerns of school board members and underwriters if such practices were engaged in today.

In numerous instances when father went to call on farm families in the valley, the boys and I retired to the woodshed where the floor boards provided an ideal arena for mumbledy-peg. In those days a good jackknife was indeed a boy's most valued possession.

* * * * *

"Play a game of Squares with me, Arnold?" Carol asked as we were finishing lunch. She had already made a grid of evenly spaced dots on the front blackboard using the yardstick to position them precisely. "I'll let you start," she offered by way of inducement.

Each participant would take a turn drawing a straight line either horizontally or vertically between the dots. The person drawing the last line which completed a square put their initial in that square to claim it. The one whose initials appeared in most squares was the winner. The contestants employed various strategies to assure their opportunities to draw that completing line.

Miss Lincoln rang the one o'clock bell for resumption of classes before we were through with our game. "Please, Miss Lincoln, can we leave the game on the board and finish it after school?" Carol pleaded. After thinking a moment about possible needs for the blackboard that afternoon, the teacher agreed with one requirement: "You two must then erase and wash the boards and clean the erasers."

When not being called up to recite, I studied the pattern on the board to plan my strategy. My preparation paid off, for, when the squares were counted, I won by a small margin. I disliked breathing the chalk dust which was a normal part of beating the erasers together outside. But winning from Carol, who was older and one of the best players, more than offset this brief inconvenience.

One common characteristic of the games we played was the simplicity of the materials needed. Without electricity or computers, we were forced to use our own ingenuity to come up with interesting activities. The joyous shouts and peals of laughter ringing out from the little white schoolhouse in the valley proved to anyone listening that we did have fun.

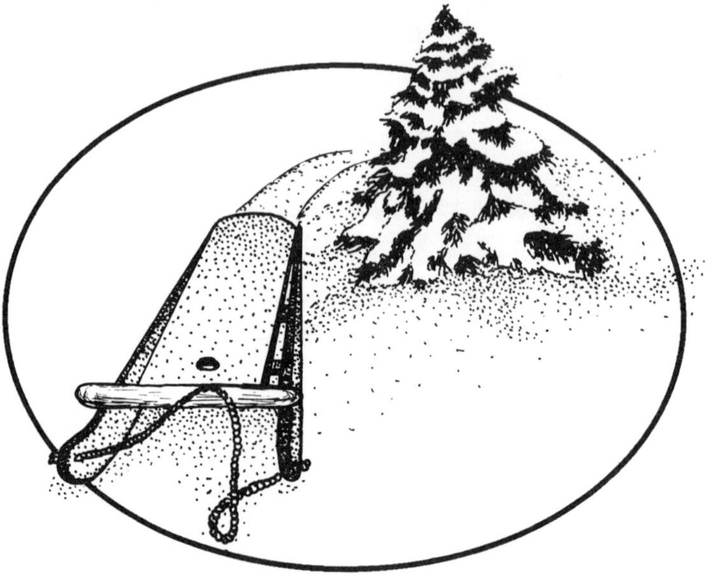

A Shaky Start, But a Speedy Finish

Trudging to school one October morning, I was startled when Clair Woodard shouted a warning as he wobbled past me on a funny-looking bicycle. Catching up with him at school, I joined the others who had clustered around him to examine his new acquisition. Even in that day, the bike had an old-fashioned appearance. Its thirty inch wheels with narrow tires put the rider high in the air while the very small, springless seat offered little comfort. But he and his brother Clinton were elated to be the first at our school to have a bike, even though they had to share it.

Proud of their new acquisition, they offered the chance to ride to any who were interested. Simultaneously I was eager to try and fearful of making a fool of myself. Desire won out. "Let me try," I begged Clair.

Holding the bike upright next to the front step of the school, Clair said: "Climb on." The pedal shanks were so long that my feet would touch the pedals during only part of their revolution. Clair shoved, setting the machine in motion, and I pedaled away, weaving wildly across the school yard and into the road. Since I couldn't reach the ground with my feet, it was either ride or fall. I was afraid to fall.

At the church corner, I turned east onto the pavement where the bike picked up speed. Clair and Clinton were way behind in the pursuit of their precious bike which was not equipped with brakes of any kind. This couldn't go on forever.

"Ride into the ditch," they shouted. Glued to the handlebars, my fingers finally responded. The left pedal caught the sod at the edge of the ditch. Over I went in a heap without one shred of dignity. Disentangling myself from the bike, I examined the places that hurt. A nasty bruise on one leg and a brush burn on my arm summed up total damages. The sturdy old bike was unscathed.

Pushing the bike back up the road, I was met by the concerned owners. Sweat running down his cheeks, Clinton exploded, "We thought you weren't ever going to stop." In spite of this awkward and scary start, the desire to have a bike of my own became a consuming passion. I was hooked on riding, as this was an activity where normal feet were not a requisite.

On father's restricted income, I well knew that getting a new bike was out of the question. When I waxed eloquent on the subject of a used one, he responded: "But you have a wagon and a scooter and a tricycle." Not only were these old, but I had practically outgrown them. How could father even compare things which were so unlike in form and function?

"Father, did you see Don's new bike?" I inquired hopefully.

"Yes. It's really a nice one," he admitted. Painted a bright red and sporting twenty-six inch balloon tires and a headlight, I thought nothing could be finer.

"Will you really try to find me a used one?" I continued my ardent campaign. This he agreed to do.

After some inquiry, father heard that Roy Shaw in Cattaraugus still had his old bike after having gotten a new one for his paper route. I gave father no rest until we went to look at the retired unit.

My first view of its dusty frame and rusty fenders might have been described as interest but hardly love at first sight. The deteriorated tires were flat and the frame was broken at the crossbar.

It certainly was not in mint condition. The blacksmith was able to braze the frame. Father bought two new tires and tubes. With a can of red paint, I covered its many scars. But I did have a bicycle of my own. As it turned out, it was the only one I ever owned as a boy.

* * * * *

"Mother. I'm going out to slide before I do my chores." "Be careful," she admonished as usual, for sledding in winter for me had proved to be a more dangerous pastime than riding a bicycle.

December days were short, leaving little opportunity for fun between the time I got home from school and daily chores. Grabbing my sled, I started for the road. A small grade descended from our house to the Brooklyn bridge. The snow, packed hard by passing vehicles, had been topped off by some freezing rain. It seemed just perfect for sliding. Holding my sled in both hands, I ran as fast as I could and then took a belly-flop, all actions calculated to gain forward momentum. I made a fast take-off.

I had failed to observe a spot part way down the hill where snow scarcely covered the pavement. When the runners hit this exposed surface, the sled stopped instantly. Inertia caused me to continue my forward movement without the sled. My face became the main point of contact, much to the detriment of my nose, forehead, chin, and teeth. Stunned for the moment, I lay sprawled in the road until the pain in my face became severe. The lenses of my glasses had shattered, cutting my face. Picking up the mangled frames, I stumbled back to the house, dragging my sled. Mother had heard me coming.

"Arnold, what did you do?" she cried.

Without waiting for an explanation, she used the limited first aid supplies available to remove bits of broken glass from my chin and cheeks, cleansed my scraped face, and applied Cloverine Salve before bandaging the area. Not one word was said about chores that evening. Since my face swelled up grotesquely, I was the center of interest when I went to school the next day. Without my glasses, doing schoolwork was difficult.

In time, all except my teeth returned to normal. The glasses had to be completely replaced, as the frames were twisted beyond repair. Although very painful, I'm sure that the physical discomfort for me was not greater than my remorse at causing my parents the financial pain for new glasses.

The Cadillac of sleds was without challenge the Flexible Flyer, due to its superior steering capability. Don had one. So did Preston and Hank. They could turn a corner with ease while my sled went into the ditch, unresponsive to my guidance. I strongly envied the owners of these maneuverable machines. Only recently, at a yard sale, I finally realized my dream of ownership. For one paltry dollar, I took title to a very old and tired specimen. It is now awaiting restoration in my basement.

* * * * *

"Come see what Dad and Grandpa are making me," Don urged the moment I arrived for a Saturday afternoon of play. In the farm shop a new bobsled was under construction. The two sets of bobs or runners were fashioned from tough oak banded with steel to provide a durable contact surface. The rear set of runners was attached to a plank over a foot wide and eight feet long. The front set of runners was pivoted so it could be turned. The driver steered by pulling on a rope attached to the point of each runner. He steadied himself by placing his boots on a footrest at the front of the plank. A narrow handrail on each side provided a handhold for the passengers.

"Where did you get the wood?" I wanted to know.

"From trees in our woods," Don replied. "We took them to the sawmill to be cut. When they were cured, we had the boards planed."

"What about the irons on the runners?" I persisted.

"They're old teeth from the hay rake. The blacksmith in East Otto shaped them for us."

Lloyd Sprowl, Don's father, was applying a coat of dark green paint to the plank. "It will be ready by the time the first snow comes," he promised.

Our impatience was rewarded when an early storm dumped several inches of snow - enough to thoroughly cover the dirt road with a packed surface. Don had plenty of company breaking in the new bobs, which held six or seven children. Packed tightly, each rider held the legs of the person behind him.

"Shove off," Don called. The last boy pushed vigorously and then attempted to hop on to the back of the moving bobsled.

Daily my desire grew to have a bobsled of my own, for with ownership went the right to steer. Without proper boards or a shop in which to work on it, I realized acquiring one wouldn't be easy. But my eagerness could not be contained.

At supper one evening, I asked: "Father, do you think there is any way I could get a bobsled?"

To my surprise, his answer was a tentative, "I'll keep my eyes open and do some inquiring." In his role as pastor, father made many calls on parishioners over quite an area. A few weeks later, he announced on returning from Cattaraugus, "I heard of a bobsled which we can get for nothing if its even worth fixing."

"Where?" I wanted to know.

"At Myrtie Freeborn's place over on Lovers Lane. It's one her grandchildren, Sanford and Beatrice, used to have."

As we pulled it out from under a pile of boards in the yard, I could see it was in deplorable condition. Two of the wooden runners were split, the footrest was smashed, and the handrails were broken. I helped father load it into our old trailer to bring it home. Father located an old oak board from his small hoard which was stashed in the barn. He sawed out two new runners and had the blacksmith shape the old irons to fit. After we replaced the rails and footrest, I applied two coats of scarlet paint and spent hours trying to shine up the rusty runner irons until they shone. For me, the period of reconstruction had dragged, although I was happy with this resurrected version. Then I had to wait over a week for snow enough to pull my bobs over to show Don and to try it out. I was delighted to find my bobsled was as long as his.

Hammond Hill, rising sharply from the Pratt Homestead, was both steep and fairly long. This was prior to the time when the road department cut the grade back to its present level. It was convenient for Don to have the best sledding slope practically at his front door. In those days the road was neither sanded nor salted, although sometimes town trucks did some plowing of snow. Horse-drawn bobsled tracks firmed the surface as farmers transported loads of logs for fuel or took grain to the mill in East Otto to be ground for feed.

Two main hazards of this course were the curve at the bottom of the hill and its intersection with West Road at the same spot. Arriving at this junction at the same moment as a vehicle was an exciting and dangerous possibility. Some very close calls were inevitable, collision being avoided only by running into the ditch. Ice on the hill increased speed at the same time control diminished. Under ideal sliding conditions, we whizzed past Pratts, clattered on past the school and church, and even continued on the county road almost to Gene Wing's place on the opposite side of the valley.

Although crude by Olympic standards, we were able to roughly determine our speeds. Stationing two adults a measured distance apart on the hill, watches carefully synchronized, we calculated approximate speed from these readings. Some of our descents were clocked at over forty miles per hour.

Sliding at night carried with it a special sense of exhilaration accompanied by increased danger, for keeping on the road became more difficult. I tried fastening a flashlight to my bobsled, but the pitifully dim beam was useless and the batteries quickly failed. Batteries did cost scarce money. Nights with a full moon were best. One advantage of night sliding was that the lights of vehicles on the highway offered better warning of their approach than during daylight.

My first attempts to devise brakes were unsuccessful. A hand-brake which forced a pointed rod into the ground created almost no response. I finally came up with loops of chain which could be dropped down over the points of the rear runners. The weight of the loaded sled plus its forward motion forced the chains back and into the icy or snowy surface, effectively slowing and stopping the bobs. However, they were useful only in an emergency. Once the chains were released, the brakes could be inactivated only by stopping the bobsled and sliding them back up out of contact. Yet, in several emergencies, they proved to be a valuable accessory for averting disaster.

For me, this innovation was of special importance as it was one feature which Don's bobsled did not have. Our competitive urge expressed itself in numerous races down Hammond Hill. Over the long run, neither of us gained a clear winning edge. Both shared the distinction of having the fastest bobsleds in the valley.

An Explosive Situation

Except for Christmas, no day stood out on the calendar like the Fourth of July. Weeks in advance of the date, I had saved every penny and nickel towards the purchase of fireworks. With sacrificial understanding, Father supplemented my slim horde before my trip to the store. Standing first on one foot and then the other, I shuttled back and forth between the counters on which were displayed all manner of creations designed to produce sound or light or both. All of this was perfectly legal, for laws banning private display of fireworks had not then been placed upon the statute books of New York State.

I first chose several packs of firecrackers. At ten cents per pack of fifty, these were basic - producing many bangs for the money. For a real blast, I next picked out some powerful-looking cherry bombs covered with flecks of shiny dust. Then came a dozen torpedoes, which exploded when thrown vigorously against the concrete. Rockets, Roman candles, pinwheels, and fountains were relatively expensive, so I had to settle for only three items among these exciting groups. One was an aerial bomb, to be reserved for the finale. Several rolls of "Big Red" caps for my cap pistol were classified in my mind as necessities. Sparklers were for sissies, little kids, and girls.

Twice I calculated the total of the items I had selected with so much care. I added three more torpedoes, completely wiping out my savings. After I had placed them on the well-worn counter, Mrs. Satterlee confirmed the accuracy of my arithmetic and quite obligingly threw into the bag several sticks of punk to be used in lighting the fuses.

As we drove the three miles home, I peered into my bag several times, savoring in anticipation the joys to come. Daily, in advance of the Fourth, I examined my hoard like a miser counting his gold. I planned how I could make my limited collection last through the day and into the night.

In July, dawn came early to our valley. But I had been awake long before sunrise. The instant the sun peeked over Mock Hill, I threw up the window sash in my bedroom, leaned out, and aimed a torpedo at the concrete walk leading out from the porch. In my excitement, I missed completely. The torpedo fell into the wet grass. The next one struck with a modest bang. Then I hurried down to retrieve the one that missed so I could dry it out on the kitchen range before it disintegrated. The Fourth of July had exploded into a glorious day.

Breakfast this morning was an interruption to be endured. I could scarcely wait until devotions were over to get on with my plans. Out on the porch I carefully untwined my packs of firecrackers into singles. Lighting them one or two at a time stretched out the fun. I never allowed myself the luxury of lighting an entire pack at once, letting them explode like popcorn over a hot fire.

Seeking greater excitement, I placed a cherry bomb under an empty pork and beans can. After lighting the exposed fuse, I quickly withdrew to a respectful distance. With a sharp crack, it sent the can soaring high above the big elm tree by the barn. The blast had caused the bottom of the can to bulge in a convex arc.

Not content with this arrangement, I located a two-foot length of half-inch pipe which had a cap screwed on one end. Into the end of the cap I drilled a hole just large enough to push through the fuse.

Recognizing some of the potential danger, I attached this crude cannon to the corner of the barn. With a firecracker attached to the fuse, I filled the open end of the pipe with old ball bearings or pebbles. Gingerly I touched the smoldering punk to the fuse, which started to sizzle. Before I could retreat very far, the device detonated with a thud. The contents of the barrel sailed far out into the meadow. The very real possibility that the pipe might shatter into jagged pieces like shrapnel never occurred to me as I repeated the experiment with several variations.

The day passed in a haze of smoke and noise. Not for anything would I show my mother my hand. One firecracker had failed to go off. After waiting what I thought to be sufficient time, I started to pick it up. Just at that instant, it exploded, singeing the hair on my right arm and burning my fingers. Fuses burned with varying speed, as I was reminded that afternoon. I lit a firecracker and was in the process of throwing it off Brooklyn Bridge. It exploded prematurely just after it left my hand. The concussion startled me. Then my whole hand tingled with pain and swelled up. I suddenly assumed a degree of caution that parental admonitions had failed to impart.

"Father, is it time to bring in the cows for milking?" I asked.

Startled that this initiative should have come from me, he pulled out his Elgin watch and stared at the time. "It's only four o'clock. It's over an hour too soon." Then, recognizing the cause for my abnormal zeal, he assured me: "Don't worry. We'll leave in plenty of time to see the fireworks."

The best of home displays paled beside the one exhibited at the Gowanda State Hospital on the evening of the Fourth. Free to the public, it attracted families from a wide radius. I kept Father informed about the time and was more cheerfully helpful than usual in assisting with chores. The old Chevy was not to be hurried as it covered the twenty-five miles between Brooklyn and Gowanda. Joining the lively crowd which had assembled, we spread a heavy horse blanket on the ground and took up the vigil as we waited for darkness.

A dull thud preceded the starburst in the sky which was punctuated by the blast from an aerial bomb. In glorious procession came giant pinwheels, multi-colored Roman candles, spewing fountains with varied hues, and the lighting of the skies with stars, rockets, and explosive flashes. Far too soon I realized from the crescendo of starbursts and the thunder of aerial bombs that the finale had come. The silence was almost deafening as we found our way to the parked car.

Although the hour was late when we arrived home, I insisted on shooting off the remainder of my salute to independence. My one rocket was cradled in a wooden trough propped up in the wheelbarrow. With high anticipation, I struck a match and touched it to the fuse. The rocket flared briefly, spurted feebly a dozen or so feet into the air before falling lifeless into the grass by the ditch. Having just experienced the marvelous exhibition at Gowanda, I sensed bitter disappointment.

"Off to bed now," Father called. "Tomorrow is another day."

That night I finally dropped off to sleep dreaming of how next year I might achieve bigger and better bangs for my buck.

* * * * *

In our rural community, work filled the long daylight hours of summer leaving the evenings short. In contrast, short days and early darkness made the winter evenings extra long. Inexpensive pastimes took a variety of forms in those Depression years.

Supper and dishes finished, we followed mother as she carried the lighted kerosene lamp into the living room. The frigid air crept in through the various cracks to remind us that the thermometer stood at ten below zero. The crackling fire in the Round Oak heater attracted father and grandma to rocking chairs close by its comforting warmth. Mother, Irving, and I gravitated to the limited circle of yellow light cast by the oil lamp.

Just as I had gotten out my arithmetic homework, mother exclaimed, "I hear something coming up the road."

Almost in unison, we all hurried to the windows and peered through the frosted glass, blowing on it to clear a peephole. The almost full moon reflected by the snow lit up the wintry scene. Down the road from the direction of the church a car moved along at moderate speed. Behind it, clutching a big rope, sped two figures on skis. In those days, ski lifts and groomed slopes were substituted for in this manner.

"There goes one down," mother noted. "I hope he isn't injured." An unseen ditch and a barbed wire fence had caused him to let go of the rope to avoid collision with them.

"He's getting up," father remarked as the downed skier rose to brush the snow from his clothing.

The old car had halted and backed up to retrieve the lost half of its daring crew. In a flurry of powdered snow, car and skiers resumed their moonlight tour of the countryside. After that glimpse into a daring activity, I found it difficult to concentrate on my arithmetic lesson. In my dreams that night I was weaving in and out from road to fields holding tight to a rope pulled by a speeding car. On my way to school the next morning, I noted the ski tracks along the way and dreamed the impossible dream - that I would ski - with feet and ankles like mine!

The snow which had fallen all day tapered off at nightfall. Lamplight from houses around the valley glimmered like markers on one of those illuminated maps at a National Park visitor center. Brimming milk pail in one hand and lantern in the other, father announced as he came into the kitchen, "Eva, I think we should make a call tonight."

I turned the cream separator more willingly than usual at the prospect of going visiting. An evening of conversation with neighbors was for us a pleasant pastime but for father an integral part of his pastoral duties. Calling ahead to see if it would be convenient was not a part of social protocol, as telephones were very scarce. A visitor to the farm homes of that day was always welcome.

Supper over, father announced, "Let's go to Steinbars." Donning heavy jackets and boots, we followed father as he led the way, breaking trail through the knee-deep snow. By far the shortest route lay directly over the fields which lay between the two roads. As he was prone to do, father sang two verses of "The Old Rugged Cross" as we progressed towards their lighted window.

Mrs. Steinbar greeted us at the woodshed door. "Chris is still in the barn," she explained. Father went off to lend a hand at finishing chores. Mother joined Mrs. Steinbar in the kitchen while Preston and I retired to the woodshed where mumbledypeg kept us occupied until time to leave. Carol, who was older than I, helped to keep Irving, my little brother, occupied and happy so the adults could talk.

When we went to visit Pratts and Sprowls who lived together as an extended family, Don and I often retired to another room to play the old Edison gramophone. The speaker was a large funnel-like horn from which the sounds emerged in raspy tones reproduced from cylindrical Bakelite cylinders. The speed from the hand-wound machine was not constant and the old cylinders were worn and scratched from much use. However, our enjoyment was unaffected by such details as lack of fidelity. Our favorite numbers were comic monologues delivered by a character known as Uncle Josh. We thought the jokes were hilariously funny no matter how many times we replayed them. In some ways they were forerunners of Garrison Keillor's "News From Lake Wobegon."

Among the popular inexpensive crafts was hooking rugs. Burlap feed bags were readily available. Designs were stamped or drawn on the burlap which was held taut on a wooden frame. The operator used a rug hook to pull appropriately colored heavy strands of yarn through the material to create a pattern or picture.

"Let's call on Ward Bergholtz," father suggested. "He's been having a hard time and can't work." We slogged through the mud which had replaced the snow on the fields, following a lane which in earlier days had been intended as a highway.

Mildred, Ward's wife, met us at the door and ushered us into the living room. Ward sat with his leg cushioned on a pillow. In those days the town hired farmers with teams and wagons to haul gravel to repair the roads in the spring. The gravel bank had collapsed, pinning his leg against the wagon and severely injuring his knee. Available medical care had not seemed to be of much assistance in restoring use of the leg. To occupy himself, Ward had taken up hooking rugs for a pastime.

"Let's see what you're working on," mother requested.

Proudly Ward spread out a scene featuring a snow-capped peak and a stream flowing among pine trees. He had just started to work on another design depicting a ferocious lion.

"You ought to enter the large one in the contest the East Otto Grange is having," mother encouraged him.

"I'm planning to," he replied, visibly pleased.

After inquiring about progress in treating the knee, father offered prayer before we took our leave. Their sons, Dick and Bob, were more nearly my brother's age, so I preferred watching Ward working on his rug to playing with the "little kids." I wondered how a farm hand with fingers so calloused from heavy work could create such expressions of beauty.

* * * * *

"What is the world coming to?" Nellie Pratt exploded, looking up from "The Cattaraugus Times" which had just arrived in the mail. Outrage showed in both her face and her voice.

"Tell me about it," father responded. He had stopped by for a brief call as he picked me up from playing with Don.

"The Methodist Episcopal Church has scheduled a jigsaw puzzle party to follow prayer meeting on Thursday evening." She held up the offending article for father to read for himself.

Agreeing generally with her concerns, he remarked: "Keeping one's mind on prayer while wondering who will win the contest would be distracting for most people. I'm sorry to see this happening. It's another sign of the times."

Indeed it was a sign of the times - difficult Depression days with money scarce for any type of recreational activities. The jigsaw puzzle had come into its own. Inexpensive puzzles were given away as incentives to purchase toothpaste or other products. Lockport-made Tuco puzzles, die-cut with sturdy backing and interlocking pieces, set the standard for quality.

An informal network for exchanging puzzles sprang up quite spontaneously, as the puzzle craze affected adults as much as their children. Speed in assembling a given puzzle became the criterion in judging contests. The size of the puzzles continued to grow from two hundred pieces to over a thousand. Some of these larger completed pictures were deemed too beautiful to be dumped back into a box, but instead were glued to a cardboard, framed, and decorated the walls of many a home.

While the popularity of this economical form of individual or group entertainment attained a very high level, never was a puzzle party made a part of the Thursday evening prayer service at the little Free Methodist Church in Brooklyn Valley.

Great Shades of Izaak Walton and Tom Sawyer

Running water has always held a high degree of fascination for boys. In the Brooklyn valley two small streams converged behind the parsonage. Cutting its way through the hills, the merged flow joined another stream originating south of Ashford Hollow to create Cannoiserauley Creek. In turn this became a tributary of the Cattaraugus Creek which entered Lake Erie at Sunset Bay.

The branch of the creek with which I was most involved started with springs up Bowen Hollow way. Gathering volume while traversing the Steinbar pasture, it meandered through the parsonage pasture lot and under the highway at Brooklyn Bridge. I knew every twist and turn of its course as it gurgled over the gravel bars and slipped silently through the deeper stretches.

It was Saturday! School was out for the summer. This June day seemed created for something special. I pedaled my bike over to

Don's house. "Let's build a dam on the creek," I urged.

"Great idea," he agreed.

"Can you get some feed bags to fill with gravel?"

"I'll see."

He emerged from the granary with an armful of sacks and some binder twine. We tied these supplies to the bike carriers and hurried to the parsonage.

"Irving. Would you like to help us with the dam?"

Happy to be included, he agreed to assist.

We chose a point where the water was naturally deeper. Firm banks on both sides of the stream made impoundment of the water possible.

"Irving, you hold the bag while Don and I shovel gravel," I ordered. From past experience we had learned how heavy bags of wet gravel could be. Filling the bags at the spot where they were to be used made the task much easier. We tied each filled bag with binder twine and pushed it tightly into place.

When Irving tired of holding the bags, we took turns encouraging him: "Just three more to go," Don reported. "You're too little to shovel."

By this time it became apparent that we would be short of bags. "I'll go ask father for some," I offered.

When I located him, father was working on his Sunday sermons. "We're building a dam and have run out of bags," I explained. "Don's grandpa gave us some, but we need five more to finish it," I begged.

"They're worth five cents each," he reminded me. This was a familiar fact and frequent repetition had burned it into my consciousness.

"Don't you have some with holes in them?" I persisted.

"Let's go look at what are hanging over the feed box." We sorted out five which could be fixed by tying up the holes. Back to the creek I hurried.

"That does it," Don said as we forced the last bag tightly into the gap to stem the flow. The porosity of the gravel didn't totally seal off the water, but permitted some of it to seep through, obviating the need for a spillway.

Already in our bathing suits, we could scarcely wait to try out the swimming hole. Don jumped in first and I followed immediately. At the deepest point the water came only up to our waists. Although hardly deep enough for real swimming, we went through the motions.

"I'm frozen," I admitted. We crawled up onto a warm rock. Don's teeth chattered and his legs were covered with goose bumps as he soon joined me. Most of the flow was water from cold springs, so its temperature was far below the comfort level.

Perched on the bank in the sun, trying to warm up after submersion in the pool, I had an idea. "Let's build a raft," I suggested, This wasn't a unique thought, as I had been reading Mark Twain's narratives of Tom Sawyer and Huck Finn.

"Let's get some of the old posts and boards from behind the barn," I ventured.

Irving and Don helped me to lug them down to the creek. Armed with an old hammer and some rusty spikes, we nailed together a rough-looking replica of a raft. After laboriously shoving it into the water, I generously offered to be first aboard. After all, it had been my idea. Maneuvering it near the bank, Don and Irving tried to join me.

"Irving, get off. It's sinking, " I cried.

Even the combined weight of two of us made it sink. So Don and I had to take turns at being simultaneously captain and crew. After pleading in vain on the bank for "My turn," Irving disappeared in the direction of the house.

Soon we admitted the obvious - the pool was too small to do much more than turn the raft around.

"Let's use the raft to make a diving board," was Don's better idea.

After dismantling the raft, we fashioned a rude platform from which we jumped, rather than dived. With water so shallow, real diving was out of the question.

Less than a week after the building of our dam, a heavy thunderstorm charged into the valley from the west. The storm seemed to have become entangled by the hills surrounding the valley. Back and forth it raged, all of the time venting copious rain. As the final reverberation sounded and the sun came through, arcing a rainbow over Mock Hill, I hurried down to the bridge. The muddy foaming torrent had breached the center of the dam, pushing several of the sandbags downstream. In those few minutes, nature had neutralized our mighty efforts at control the stream.

"Let's make boats after school," I suggested to Don.

"That's OK by me," he responded heartily.

The workshop at Pratts offered tools, shelter, and most of the needed materials. Part of a bundle of cedar shingles left over from a roof repair job provided the basic hulls for the boats. With a coping saw, we tapered the heavier end of the shingle to a point for a prow. Next, we cut out a rectangular section from the opposite end, leaving a large slot. Across this slot we stretched a heavy rubber band. A flat piece of shingle we inserted in the rubber band to serve as a paddle wheel.

When each of us had completed a boat, Don urged, "Let's try them out." Biking to the creek took less than five minutes. I wound the rubber bands on my boat in reverse and Don did the same.

"One. Two. Three. Start," I called.

We each released the paddles on our boats at the same moment. Down the creek they went, paddles splashing and water gurgling. As the rubber bands lost their tension, the boats slowed to a stop.

"Mine wins," Don exulted as his craft outdistanced mine by at least two feet. Back we went to the head of the pool to renew the battle of the boats until father called me for chores.

Somewhere I had seen an operating water wheel and thought a small one would be a fine addition to our fun. I envisioned running a variety of devices from the power it would generate. Lacking proper tools to build it, I enlisted Don's help.

We sawed the parts for the wheel in the shop at the Pratt farm. Between the two round sides of the wheel, we nailed the slats which caught the force of the water. Confidently we carried our creation to the stream. We supported the wheel on a steel axle between two heavy stakes.

The wheel barely turned in the slow-moving water. We lacked the resources to build a flume. Too, the level of water changed frequently. Reluctantly we abandoned this ambitious project which we had tackled with great anticipation.

"Let's go fishing," Don responded to my question about how to spend that Saturday afternoon in July.

"Great idea! Let's dig bait." In dry weather, knowing where to dig was the secret of success. Don lifted an old plank next to the pig pen while I quickly sunk the spade into the rich moist soil. I grabbed two plump worms before they could escape and dropped them into the Campbell Pork and Beans can. Had we planned in advance to go fishing, I would have picked up night crawlers from the moist lawn the night before. That would have saved both time and the work of digging.

When the can held a reasonable supply of bait, we prepared our poles. To the simple bamboo poles, we attached fish line, bobber, and hooks. Exclusive of the pole, the rest of the outfit I had purchased for fifteen cents at Russell's Hardware.

Exercising faith, I put the eight inch skillet in a bag along with a little lard in a jar, salt, matches, and a fork. Based on past experience, we wasted no time on the shallow stretches of water. Instead, we concentrated our efforts on deeper spots where the current carried the bait under snags and up underneath overhanging banks. About the only fish in the creek were various types of minnows and suckers, none of which grew very large.

"I've got one," Don called quietly with suppressed excitement. The next moment a six inch, horned dace was flopping on the bank. This was about as large as any we caught in the creek. We fished frequently enough so I'm certain none of them ever died of old age.

While Don was busy with that one, I let my worm drift out of sight beneath the same snag. After a few tentative nibbles were telegraphed along my line, I felt a solid bite. I jerked to set the hook. With steady pressure, I kept the fish from tangling the line. Grabbing my catch, slightly smaller than Don's, I placed it on the twine stringer along with the first one.

Two hours and five fish later, we sat down on a log which had washed up on a gravel bar. "If you'll clean the fish, I'll start a fire," I offered. Gathering some dry branches and bark, I soon had flames blazing up between some rocks arranged to hold the skillet. The small fish crisped up quickly.

"They sure taste good," Don pronounced.

"Right you are," I chimed in.

Looking back, I admit that the time we spent fishing was quite out of proportion to what we caught. For, more often than not, the skillet came back unused. The pure joy of spending time along a murmuring stream on a summer day was beyond calculation.

Living things in and along the stream captured our interest. We watched the schools of minnows dart about a placid pool. We noted the habits of the crabs crawling and flipping about under water in search of food. Their claws sometimes pinched a finger or bare toe. Fascinating was the movement of water skippers - those long-legged insects which could walk on the water. How we wanted to learn their secret! Sometimes we startled a muskrat, who made a dive into the stream and disappeared into his burrow under the overhanging bank. Or we startled a great blue heron standing in the creek fishing.

But the water snakes received more of our attention than any of the other creatures. They preferred the sunny abutments of Brooklyn Bridge on which to coil and sun themselves. Although not venomous, they were capable of inflicting a nasty bite which could easily become infected. The standard method of capturing them was to pin them down just behind the head with the fork of a stick. By grasping the head, we could handle them without being bitten.

Due to all that my feet had endured, the soles of them were abnormally tender. While my friends ran barefoot or walked on the gravel without discomfort, these activities for me were exceedingly painful. Without shoes, my trip down to the creek was one of carefully chosen steps, avoiding rocks and thistles.

I had decided to go down to the creek to check on the dam. When almost to the swimming hole, I saw two snakes coiled right in my path. They were larger and patterned differently from the water snakes and garter snakes with which I was familiar. Instead of slithering away, their heads and bodies swayed aggressively towards my bare feet. My scalp began to prickle and my knees began to shake. So terrified was I that I fled through the pasture and didn't stop running until I reached the house. I gave no conscious thought to where I was stepping. All of this took place without my perceiving pain in my feet. Such was the power of fear.

"Father! Mother!" I shrieked. Both of them came running.

When I had calmed down enough to tell them about the snakes, father went armed with a big hoe. I followed at a safe distance, pointing out where I had seen them. Although we searched the area, the snakes had disappeared, not to be seen again.

* * * * *

"Eva. Can you do something to keep the boys quiet?" father asked.

As usual he was trying to concentrate on his evening sermon. Playing ball and engaging in active games was not considered proper for the Sabbath. But my parents did approve of taking a walk.

"Let's go to Rockbottom," was my request. Irving seconded the idea.

Instead of following the meanderings of the creek, we crossed Brooklyn Bridge and shortly turned left down a farm lane which led almost directly to our destination.

Here at "Rockbottom" the stream had worn a deep groove through the hills, cutting its channel down to reach several strata of grey shale. This gradual process of erosion had formed cascades and chutes smooth enough to slide down. Though a bit rough on our seats, it was an early version of the modern-day water slides. The shale was soft and flaked off to continually alter the form of these delightful cascades. At the base of the last fall, where the rock stratum ended, the force of the falling water had hollowed out a fine pool for swimming. For my brother and me, this cool shady haven was the ideal place to spend a hot Sunday afternoon.

Long before we were ready, mother called out: "Come here. It's time to start back to the house."

For many years I dreamed of buying the land and building a log cabin among the hemlocks on a little plateau overlooking this boyhood retreat.

A larger and more impressive version of "Rockbotttom" had been created far downstream on Cannoiserauley Creek. The family who owned this area on the creek at the terminus of a dead-end dirt road generously permitted the public to use it for picnics and recreation. The greater volume of water plus increased thickness of the strata produced higher falls and a greater variety of formations.

Under one falls, a little cave had been formed, permitting two or three people to climb up behind the falling water. One perfectly hollowed-out spot was dubbed "the bathtub." Beneath the last cascade, hedged in on both sides by sheer shale cliffs, lay a pool of water. This was deep enough for diving and extensive enough for swimming. One deterrent was its location in this narrow defile where the sun had almost no chance to temper the chill of the spring-fed stream. In the fall, when flanked by the scarlets and yellows and lavenders of maple, poplar, and ash, I thought no scene could surpass the beauty of Cannoiserauley Falls.

* * * * *

Along the abutments of Brooklyn Bridge a large clump of elderberry bushes flourished. When they attained a stage of purple maturity, mother gathered the tiny berries, formed in a flat cluster, to make into delicious pies. Nothing in the entire world tastes like elderberry pie. But I had found another use for this plant.

"Let's make popguns," I suggested to Irving. He helped me cut several of the largest canes. The center of the coarse stalk contained a soft pithy substance. I removed sections of the stalk between two joints. The next step required mother's cooperation. Taking a piece of heavy wire and the lengths of elderberry stalks, we went to the kitchen.

"Mother, may we heat our wire in the kitchen stove so we can make popguns?" we asked. Then we added, "We'll be very careful." Her approval was less than enthusiastic.

We inserted one end of the wire into the firebox of the kitchen range, placing it on the burning coals. When the wire glowed red-hot, I forced the heated end into the stalk which my brother was holding. The odor of burning pith filled the kitchen as repeated applications of the hot wire cleared the stalk and left a hollow tube.

I chose a dowel the right size to move freely through the tube. This acted as handle and plunger. Irving shredded newspapers into a dish pan of warm water, transforming them into a pulpy mass. This was our ammunition.

"Outside!" mother ordered. How well she knew about the wads of paper that would adhere to walls and ceilings! She shooed us through the door along with our crude weapons and ammunition.

I forced one wad of paper to the end of the tube, thus sealing it. Then I started a second wad in the open end. When I quickly pushed the plunger, the compression of air ejected the first wad out with great force and a loud "pop." These outdoor wars were waged with little danger to the participants. A splat in the face from a soggy wad of paper was the worst consequence.

Another not-so-innocuous weapon for our hunting expeditions

along the creek was the slingshot. Preston and Don had their own .22 caliber rifles. Almost all other farm boys had air rifles. But the cost of these was out of my reach. With the biblical account of David's sling exploits I could relate. It cost nothing except my work.

Roaming the woods, I was always on the lookout for the perfectly shaped crotch of a tree from which to fashion a slingshot. Most boys judged hickory best for its resiliency and strength. After sawing to proper length the two forks and handle, I peeled off the bark and put it away to season.

I cut the rubber bands for the sling from old auto tubes. The stretch of this rubber far exceeded that of today's synthetics. With strong twine I bound the two strips of rubber to the matched prongs and attached the loose ends to the leather pouch.

Out in the back yard I placed a tin can on a block of wood. Selecting a smooth round stone from my supply, I nestled it in the pouch. Pulling the rubber bands back, I aimed through the V of the crotch. To my delight, the can went tumbling to the ground.

While slingshots were potentially lethal, the many parental admonitions about their use were effective. My revulsion to killing animals or birds made me confine my targets to inanimate objects in the pasture and along the stream.

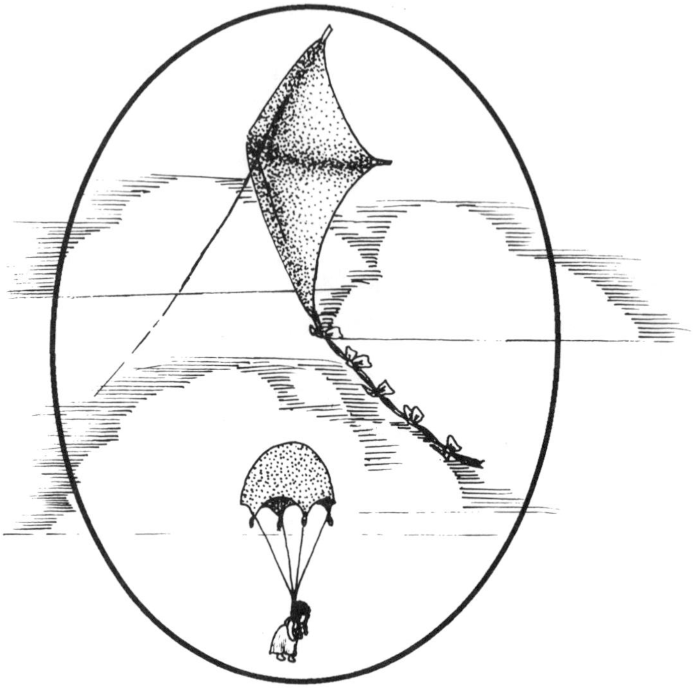

You Started It, Ben Franklin

Being literally earthbound did not remove my desire to become involved on a small scale with more lofty endeavors. Kites, with their ability to rise upon unseen breezes and look down from perspectives unavailable to boys, became the outlet for this urge. While kites could be bought at the Five and Dime stores for ten cents or so, this sum of money was only one reason for desiring something better. Their bows, sawed out of flimsy wood, often snapped under even modest stress. And the thin paper, printed in gaudy colors, easily ripped or disintegrated if wet. The answer was a do-it-yourself product with each kite unique in its individuality.

Materials for kite making were readily available: bamboo, brown wrapping paper, and string. In those days, carpeting often was shipped with a bamboo pole in the center to prevent creasing of the rugs in shipment. Friendly storekeepers gladly gave away these discarded shipping rods. Likewise, brown wrapping paper covered shipments of products such as mattresses and often were obtained in fairly large sheets. Twine was generally the only purchased item, unless one were willing to settle for salvaged lengths of "sugar string" tied end to end. Lines pieced together resulted in knots every few feet, increasing the risk of their pulling loose in flight.

For smaller kites, we split the bamboo from the round stalk into thinner staves. This part was the most difficult operation, as a slip of the knife sometimes gashed my hand or ruined the wood. Creating two bows of comparable strength was not easy using our rather crude tools.

After the ends of these bows were notched with a saw or knife, we bound the crossbows at their intersection to form the traditional kite shape. We pulled string taut as it passed around the four ends, to form the outside perimeter of the kite.

When the piece of paper was not large enough, we pasted two or more sections together with glue - either wallpaper paste or a home-made mixture of flour and water. Patience was required at this point to allow the paste to thoroughly dry after attaching the paper to the kite frame.

Placement of the bridle or lead string was critical to the kite's staying aloft. Location of its two points of attachment to the vertical bow and positioning of the loop in the bridle had much to do with whether or how well the kite would fly. We spent much time making adjustments. A bow string drew the two ends of the horizontal cross-piece back about an inch or so from the center plane in a small arc. At last the kite was ready to fly if winds cooperated.

In Brooklyn valley winds generally came from the west or northwest. One of the modern kite hazards was totally missing from the scene, as no electric wires had invaded our valley. Trees constituted the major threat. In a brisk wind, the kites took off without special help. When the breeze was gentle, we ran, pulling the kites aloft to catch air currents above ground level.

Once aloft, if perfectly balanced, the kite soared and dipped to the cadence of the breezes. Sometimes a kite would dive erratically, eventually plunging to the ground in an act of self-destruction. Adjustments of bridle and bow strings usually corrected the problem. If this wasn't successful, we attached a tail to stabilize the flight.

Don and I vied in contests to determine whose kite could fly the highest or stay up the longest. Another measure of superiority was the length of string released. The main chore was winding it all back in again in such a way that it didn't tangle. Don constructed an efficient wooden reel with a crank for faster retrieval of the string. This was important, for winds could quickly die. Down the kite would come, necessitating our walking along and winding up the string until we reached the kite.

Seeing Don's kite in the sky, I rode my bike over to his place. A steady western breeze made the string tug sharply.

"Can you let it out farther?" I wanted to know. "Can you use all of your string?"

Accepting the challenge, Don responded, "Let's try."

The reel spun and the straining kite continued to climb into the clear evening air.

Watching the revolving reel, I reported: "Just a few more turns left."

Without warning, the wind ceased as if a switch had turned off the blower. Don started cranking furiously while I tried to keep the string distributed on the reel. Our best efforts were not enough. The kite fell and so did darkness.

"Wait while I get a flashlight," Don requested as he dashed into the house. He returned with the big six-cell Ever-ready.

"You shine the light and lift up the string while I carry the reel and wind it up," he ordered.

As we crossed the south meadow, the task went smoothly. Next, a dry stream bed flanked by barbed wire fences added to the difficulty. Across the Hintz property we fought our way through a patch of briars which grabbed at the string and scratched our bare arms. With deepening darkness, the beam of the flashlight was of little help in locating the string when it was suspended high in bushes and trees.

In crossing the creek, we both stumbled on slippery unseen rocks and got soaked to the waist. In the darkness, vicious mosquitoes took advantage of the fact that our hands were occupied with our task. Suddenly the string soared high in the air over the tops of the huge sugar maples lining the road by Nelligans. Resigned to the impossibility of retrieving the string in one piece, Don cut it loose.

Noting carefully the direction in which the line pointed, we ran down the road and over into the parsonage fields. By now the flashlight had ceased to even glow. Back and forth we went, searching for the string.

Something caught on my face. "Don! I've found it," I cried.

Following its lead, we discovered the missing kite in the middle of our potato patch. The next morning passersby could catch sight of the unretrieved portion of the kite string as it waved from the tops of the big maples. For weeks it offered mute evidence of setting a kite flying record in the valley.

My claim to kite fame came later. I thought that bigger would be better, so I devised two bows six feet long from a larger-than-usual bamboo rod. The paper was extra heavy sacking and the string a much heavier twine than the usual kite string. The kite towered over my five foot stature by more than a foot. With a brisk wind blowing, I launched my creation.

The strength of its pull quickly severed the frail cord I held, and down the monster fell. Remembering a length of new light rope I had seen in the barn, I appropriated it for this worthy cause. Fighting wildly, the kite twisted and turned, plunging to the ground. It needed a tail for stability, but the usual materials didn't work. I ended up using binder twine with heavy iron nuts attached at intervals. Now it flew, but it tugged so mightily that I had to use leather gloves to avoid rope burns.

Even more memorable was the second occasion of its flight. Steinbar's herd of Holsteins was grazing placidly in their pasture adjoining the parsonage meadow. As the huge kite rose into the air, the sight of this object ducking and diving over their heads was just too much. Like a scene from the wild west, they stampeded wildly through the brush, tails lifted in the air.

Observing this moving scene, father rushed excitedly to my side shouting: "Get that thing down right now"

"Why?" I asked quite innocently.

"You've upset Steinbar's cows and that will affect their giving milk," he explained.

We never learned whether at milking time there was decreased production or milkshakes. Nevertheless father forbade my flying that kite whenever the neighbor's cows were anywhere in the vicinity. Father also insisted on the return of his rope, sending my prize kite into early retirement. I was thankful it hadn't happened before my having set the record of flying the largest kite in the valley.

Don and I sought some variations from straight kite flying. One alternative was to fasten an object to a parachute improvised from a handkerchief and some string. We wedged this load behind the vertical bow in such a way that it could be easily dislodged by jerking the string while the kite was in the air.

Tiring of using pebbles and sticks, Don asked his sister May, "Can we use one of your small dolls?" Without enthusiasm, she agreed.

With the kite aloft again, quick tugs on the kite string freed the parachute and its load. It appeared to us a life-like miniature of pictures we had seen.

"Let's try it with two kites," I suggested. Don sent May to the house to bring another doll while I created a parachute from my handkerchief.

Then competition emerged. "Let's see whose parachute comes down first," Don called.

Up the kites went and at a signal, we both jerked. Down floated the chutes, sometimes one, sometimes the other touching ground first.

With the two kites, we enlisted Ethel to help. The two girls each put an arm over one string and walked the kite to the ground. After tucking the chute and "passenger" behind the bow, they released the kites to soar again. The other part of their task was to retrieve the parachutes. This fun had gone on for some time.

Then May cried out in fear, "The parachute isn't opening."

Her doll came hurtling down, striking the ground with a dull thud. Rushing over to the point of impact, May pulled the doll from where it was imbedded in the alfalfa sod.

"Ethel. Get the other doll," she ordered. "This is much too dangerous for my dolls. We're leaving."

Our pleas went unheeded. They also were tired from doing all the chasing. "Use your own toys," May yelled. So Tootsi-Toy trucks filled in as substitutes the rest of the afternoon.

A variation on the parachute idea was to attach a balsa-wood glider to the kite and send it up. Gliders proved more difficult to fasten to the bow than parachutes in a way which didn't cause them to get out of adjustment and malfunction on the way down. When they glided as intended, the sight was thrilling to us. Other attempts brought destructive crashes as the balsa-wood gliders slammed into the ground and splintered. And they cost ten or fifteen hard-to-come-by pennies.

Don and I staged gliding contests to see whose craft could sail the farthest. An abandoned gravel pit on the Nelligan place proved to be the best test site. A knoll had been excavated on one side to form an almost vertical drop-off for launching. We ran down the gradual grade on the other side to retrieve the gliders and then trudged back up to do it again.

We devised a launcher, a stick with a large rubber band attached. We placed a hook on the underside of the glider near the front. With the rubber band in the hook, we drew the glider backwards until the tension was strong. Then we released the craft. It operated like a catapult.

The success rate was about fifty percent, as sometimes the glider didn't detach and would be jerked back. At other times, in launching, the wing of the glider would hit the arm of the person holding the launcher. In either case, the launch was aborted and the glider frequently sustained damage. This activity always had one predictable outcome: much exercise for the participants.

When an occasional plane droned over our valley, we dreamed of experiencing real flying. The contrast with our kite and glider efforts made them seem puny and futile. But we never lost the dream.

Survival!

When father took appointment to the Brooklyn church in the early throes of the Great Depression, the need to supplement the meager income from the pastorate was apparent. For five people to live (father, mother, Grandma Willis, my brother Irving, and me) required more than the approximately six dollars per week paid by the church. This sum included the monetary equivalents of contributions in the form of meat, home-canned items, and whatever people could offer. When father died, I found the account books where he had meticulously recorded all such support.

At times the amount from the church was only two or three dollars instead of the targeted amount. Some of these seven years were leaner than others, the average weekly salary varying between a low of $4.35 in 1934 and a high of $7.69 in 1931. Some of this was father's own tithe. In this he set an example for both the congregation and his family. Recognizing the poverty of most parishioners, my parents never complained. Instead, they assumed responsibility for making up, through their own efforts, whatever else was needed.

Until father attended Cleveland Bible Institute (now Malone College), he had worked for Grandfather Cook on the family farm near Elba in Genesee County. Consequently, he had a very good working knowledge of farming. Also, in his first term at Brooklyn from 1921-24, he had farmed the ten acres of land which had remained part of the parsonage property. He integrated farming on a very small scale into the work of the pastorate.

Getting started without any savings or financial reserves was an immediate challenge. With milk selling for $1.25 to $1.50 a hundredweight, dairymen often felt they couldn't afford the services of a veterinarian or take much time to nurse a sick cow. The alternative was often to kill the cow or sell it for the little a dairy cow would bring for beef.

One Sunday Frank Reed approached father after church. "Pastor, I have a cow with a bad foot and leg. If you want to fuss with doctorin' her, she's yours."

"Thank you, Brother Reed," father responded. "I'll come after her tomorrow morning."

The painful journey over the dusty road from the Reed farm to Brooklyn was agonizingly slow. The cow hobbled the two miles mainly on three legs. Anointing the hoof and leg with a nasty-looking black ointment and wrapping it in old rags, my father nursed her back to health.

Another cow we purchased for eleven dollars from a farmer in West Valley. We called her Bess, the hillside cow, as on one side the muscles supporting her udder had been damaged, causing it to hang in a lopsided manner. In addition, she had only three teats, the fourth never having developed. But she was a Jersey and gave the richest milk of any cow we ever had.

I know this because in eighth grade, when I attended East Otto Union School, part of the Ag 1 course was learning to test for butterfat. Although the other boys in the class came from farms where Holsteins produced relatively great quantities of milk, none could approach the butterfat record of old Bess. In that class I also learned the 86 parts of a cow and how to judge a good dairy animal - skills I never was called upon to use afterwards!

To compete with other farmers by producing milk didn't make any sense. Instead, father looked for a propitious niche: products for which there was a ready demand as well as those which the family could use. The answer proved to be converting the milk into butter, buttermilk, and cottage cheese. Demand from the three outlets that developed for these products soon outpaced the modest amounts we could produce.

Community people were eager to get the "good butter" that Grandma Willis churned. We soon developed regular customers for a significant share of the output. Often I was the delivery boy, exchanging full crocks of the golden substance for empty ones.

The Jewett Store in East Otto was willing to accept butter and eggs in trade for the things that couldn't be produced at home. The term, "trading at the store," has transferred into the current conversation of some older people. However, it no longer carries the sense of barter or exchange for non-monetary items. Often the price calculated for our goods determined the extent to which mother could satisfy her shopping list.

The third market consisted of more affluent people who drove "clear from Buffalo," sixty miles away, to buy, direct from the farm, butter and buttermilk that they considered to be truly outstanding. One man, who sported a big black Buick sedan, came quite regularly on alternate Saturdays. Limitations on output included the four stanchions in the small barn and forage that the small acreage could produce to feed the cows.

Without horses, the standard power source at that time, father made-do with our old 1928 Chevy auto and a homemade trailer. I learned to drive the car in the fields as father loaded hay on the trailer with a pitchfork while I maneuvered the car up to the haycocks lining the field. Lacking synchro-mesh transmission, the Chevy was not easy to shift and stalled frequently. I now realize that father's stern shouts of instructions merely reflected his concern for what it might cost to reline the clutch. With that kind of initiation to driving, neither back roads in the United States nor those in New Zealand later intimidated me.

Work that couldn't be done with the car, such as plowing, mowing hay, and cutting grain, father accomplished by borrowing a team and tools from neighbors in exchange for day labor for them. Gene

Wing, the largest farmer in the valley, owned a Fordson tractor, a steel-wheeled back-wrenching brute to drive. However, it never was used on our few acres.

Lacking a silo to store ensilage to feed the cows during the winter, father hit upon an alternative. He planted mangel beets, not your garden variety, but a kind that grew to be two or more feet long. Growing and harvesting them entailed a lot of hard work. Often they were so embedded in the soil that at harvest time we pried them out with a shovel. We knocked some of the dirt from the roots, twisted off the leafy tops, and carried the giant beets to the earthen basement under the house. Like cordwood, we stacked them up to store for winter use.

As soon as winter weather made outside grazing impossible, one of my least-liked chores became a daily trial. Right after school, my task was to bring from the basement to the barn enough beets for the cows' daily supply. Armed with a butcher knife, I knocked off as much of the remaining soil as possible and sliced the beets into pieces the cows could eat without danger of choking. I despised the sticky juice oozing from the cut beets and mingling with the dirt to coat my hands. Eager to not prolong the job, I sometimes cut pieces which father considered too large for the cows to eat safely.

"Arnold," father called. "Come back and do your job right. Do you want to choke a cow on these big chunks?"

Of course I didn't. Grudgingly I worked through the pails of cut beats, reslicing the larger portions. Doing this was messier than the original task. And I vowed to do it right next time to escape this gooey penalty.

Father seldom called on me to do the milking. I was content to abide by his decision. A few instances of my getting kicked off the three-legged milking stool by a cow who didn't appreciate my efforts had something to do with his choice. Or it may have been my losing the precious milk when the cow put her foot into the pail. Or my father may have been convinced that he could squeeze out more of this cash-producing fluid than my best efforts would extract. I welcomed freedom from being swatted by a cow's manure-matted tail and counted this one of my blessings.

One duty I carried out twice a day. Right after the milk was brought to the house, I turned the crank of the De Laval separator which, by centrifugal action, separated the cream from the milk. I found the job was more boring than difficult. Father declared: "Arnold you have two speeds - too fast and too slow." Either mode, he assured me, was detrimental to extracting the maximum amount of cream. I don't recall his ever praising me for maintaining the proper speed.

I participated in one other portion of the dairy process: churning the butter. Lacking refrigeration of any kind (we didn't even have a spring house), we accumulated the cream in covered containers. Mother stored these in the relative coolness of the cellar until there was enough to churn.

I used a traditional churn with a dasher moved up and down by hand when the amount of cream was relatively small. For larger batches, a barrel churn was more efficient. The wooden barrel-like container, suspended on an upright frame, was turned by a handle. Whichever churn was chosen, I was the assigned motive power. Never was I entrusted with doing this alone. Grandma Willis supervised the entire operation.

Again, my problem was with the speed with which I worked the dasher or turned the barrel churn. According to grandma, it took the right amount of agitation to "make the butter come." My turning the barrel churn too fast caused the cream to be held against the bottom by centrifugal force instead of sloshing and cascading down on itself. In time, the truth that turning the churn faster actually took longer to accomplish its purpose tempered my cranking speed.

In the churning process, gas was generated. This was released by stopping the barrel and opening the bung or cork in the top of the churn. Failing to release this pressure periodically caused the bung to pop out and splatter cream all over. With grandma's close supervision, this seldom happened. She could tell when the butter was about "ready to come" and took over at this critical phase.

Except on very cold winter days, the churning took place in the dank cobwebby basement with a dirt floor. This transformation from a liquid to a semi-solid was carried out by the dim light of a kerosene lantern or lamp which cast eerie shadows on the rough walls. This was the setting for what then seemed at the time to be a major disaster.

"Arnold. Go down cellar and turn the churn for Grandma."

Mother's call brought me back from reading *The Shepherd of the Hills* to real life on the farm.

Grandmother was waiting to supervise me as I turned the barrel churn with its monotonous swish-glug. Periodically she had me stop so she could unscrew the fastening on the lid, open the churn, and examine the contents to assess its progress. In the meantime, I held the churn steady to keep it from turning upside down.

Then it happened! After one of these inspections, I started to turn the crank. As the churn reached the upside-down position, the cover, which had apparently not been tightened properly, fell off and the entire batch of cream poured out over the earthen floor. I was too astonished to keep turning and bring it upright, so the entire contents was lost.

"Eva! Eva! Come quickly!" grandma called to mother.

From the kitchen mother appeared almost instantly. Taking in the calamity at a glance, mother rushed out to the front porch crying: "Elmer! We need you immediately."

From where he had been mixing feed in the barn, father came dashing down into the cellar. Surveying the mess, father resorted to his habitual evaluation appropriate to such extremities: "Blessed be nothing!" he moaned. This pithy statement should not be confused with one of the Beatitudes.

Attracted by the commotion, Irving appeared down the cellar hatch to see what trouble I had brought upon myself. Into the midst of this tense family gathering stalked our three-colored cat. After surveying this unusual scene, the cat nonchalantly began to lap up the cream which was rapidly soaking into the bare earthen floor.

I felt that my moment of doom had arrived. Grandma accepted the responsibility for the mishap, but I felt father's disapproval of my contributory negligence. This batch of cream had been unusually large, so the seriousness of this misfortune fanned out in two directions. First, customers would not get their promised butter. Second, the financial loss of three days' production by the cows would affect necessary purchases for the family.

As I recall, we didn't use any butter ourselves for some time until this shortage was made up. That was no sacrifice for me, as my working with the various parts of the milk process had made both the smell and sight of milk, butter or cottage cheese distasteful. To this day, I still loathe cottage cheese because of smelling it "making" on the back of the warm kitchen range.

Mercifully I was allowed no part in the final processes of butter-making, although I was familiar with the activity. The buttermilk was drained off into containers to be sold, or was fed to the pigs (to my mind, a fitting use!) The curds of butter grandma collected into one large yellow lump. Mother then took over and "worked" the butter on a board by pressing a butter paddle through it to remove any remnants of moisture. She next added a proper amount of salt, working it evenly into the plastic yellow mass. In the winter, she sometimes added butter coloring.

Selecting the appropriate earthenware butter crocks, each pre-weighed with the weight written in pencil on the bottom, she filled them with one or two pounds of the golden product. Mother often displayed a touch of artistry by creating a fancy design on the surface of the butter. After carefully covering it with waxed paper, mother took it down to the basement to cool. Finally, Cook's butter was ready to distribute to the customers in and beyond our valley.

Rampaging Pigs and Smoked Chickens

Grandma's pride and joy was her flock of Bantam chickens, usually three or four hens and a rooster, a cocky little fellow who announced with his shrill crow the coming of each new day. What eggs were laid appeared as miniatures with limited nutritional value.

Apparently having this little brood clucking around the yard and garden reminded her of the home in Ireland which she left as a girl of sixteen during the potato famine. She landed in Boston where she served as nanny for the children of a wealthy family. After repaying the cost of her passage, she saved money from her earnings to bring her two sisters to the United States.

One feature for which the little brown hens were noted was setting on the nest to incubate a brood of chicks. Father wanted to get started with a "real laying flock" to provide not only eggs for home use but to supplement family income. When one of the Bantam hens displayed setting behavior, father obtained some fertile eggs from another farmer's Leghorn flock and substituted them for the pee-wees. The bantam didn't seem to mind the substitution and may even have been elated to set on a clutch of large eggs. In this way we developed a small flock of laying hens. Father built a chicken coop and fenced yard to assure the containment of the chickens and the collection of their output.

The next spring father decided to quickly increase the flock through ordering by mail 100 baby chicks from a hatchery. One chilly day in early April, the mailman delivered a square flat box from which a persistent peeping sound emerged. Father had obtained a used brooder - a cone-like metal hood with a little oil stove in the center to keep the chicks warm. Maintaining an even temperature proved to be a problem. The oil burner, of the wick variety, had a propensity for going out, especially if we left home for any reason. As a result, most of the time, except during church services, someone had to stay home to keep checking on the chicks.

The perverse little creatures demonstrated some self-destructive habits. Whether for warmth or companionship, they tended to crowd together into a heap. Unless forcibly dispersed, the ones on the bottom were trampled and smothered to death. In retrospect, this quirk was remarkably similar to the actions of spectators at a British soccer championship meet!

Another anti-social behavior was their cannibalizing of any weak member who was ill and unable to fend for itself. Some chicks always died from these known causes as well as from unexplained sources. To guard against disease, we dissolved Walko tablets in their drinking water which turned it a lurid purple. Fortunately, this infant stage was of relatively short duration.

Mother often took weak chicks into the kitchen, placing them in a box with a hot water bottle or a jar filled with warm water and wrapped with a towel. This peeping of chicks in the kitchen was not a phenomenon confined to Easter weekend. When they became lively enough to surmount the screen barrier propped in the doorway of the kitchen and escaped to the living room, mother decreed them ready to rejoin their peers in the brooder house. Her sense of cleanliness won out over the tender heart she had towards all living creatures. A reasonable number of chicks reached maturity in spite of the numerous life-threatening hazards to which they might have fallen prey.

One morning, while we were at breakfast, the milk truck screeched to a halt in front of our house. Edwin Fleckenstein, the driver, ran up the walk and banged on the door. As soon as father opened the door, Edwin delivered the startling news: "Smoke is pouring out of your brooder house."

Immediately father rushed to the rescue with the rest of the family in hot pursuit. Grandma and our inquisitive cat brought up the rear. As father swung open the door, billows of sooty black smoke poured out. The oil burner had started to soot up, filling the shed with oily, black particles.

Grabbing some feed bags, father smothered the sooty flames and cleared the smoke from the shed by opening all of the windows and doors. Most important of all, the chicks had survived this premature barbecue with surprisingly little harm.

But one remarkable transformation had occurred. During those few moments, the naturally White Leghorns had changed to a sooty gray tint which they retained until their feathers grew out. Father received a lot of good-natured kidding from neighbors about his white Leghorns turning a tattle-tale gray.

Father's choice of Leghorns was due to their reputation for high egg production. Another of their characteristics was not so admirable: their prowess in flying. Keeping them fenced in was a challenge. We all soon got tired of chasing the high fliers. In spite of mother's pleas, eventually father reduced the number of fugitives by clipping the feathers on one wing, upsetting their aerodynamic balance. Until they accepted this modification of their plumage, Irving and I were highly amused by their air-show acrobatics as they tried to scale the fence.

Feeding the chickens and collecting the eggs were chores I enjoyed. But I despised the smelly task of periodically cleaning out the hen manure and creosoting the roosts to combat lice. Every excuse or delay I could conceive of was employed, but to no avail. The acrid odors of chicken droppings and creosote I perceived as offensive assaults on my organs of smell.

Nor was cleaning the cow stable high on my scale of preferred chores, although this was a twice-a-day necessity. Getting the manure from the barnyard to the fields meant twice more dealing with the same materials. While father might help in loading the trailer, he chose to drive in the field because only he had the special knowledge of where the land was yearning for its fertilizing richness. My post was to stand on the trailer and wield the manure fork in response to father's shouted instructions.

Winter added the heavy burden of bringing water to the cows. When the creek was frozen over, the temperatures were too bitter, or the snows were too deep to let the cows outside, I had to bring water for them to drink. From the pump in the shed attached to the house, I carried the water in pails across the road to the barn. To keep up milk production, providing them with all of the water they wanted was imperative. When I was in a special hurry, their thirst seemed insatiable.

When a cow became ill, father went to the friendly veterinarian for advice and medication, which was far cheaper than having him come and administer it.

"Brownie's sick," father explained when I arrived home from school, hoping for a little sledding before chores. "I'll need your help in the barn."

Not eagerly anticipating this change of plans, I quickly switched from my corduroys into barn jeans before joining father in the stable. Our Brown Swiss mooed and was obviously suffering.

"You hold her head," father ordered. "Keep it pointed up so medicine will run down her throat."

Cows, especially sick cows, never take kindly to having their heads held in awkward positions. On the first attempt, Brownie jerked her head free.

"Grab her ears and pull back," father suggested.

My success was momentary. Just as father had inserted into her mouth the pop bottle holding the medicine, she belched mightily. This blast spewed the dark mixture into father's face and trickled down the sleeve of my jacket.

Wiping the medicine from his face, father grunted: "Didn't get any inside. Let's try again."

After two more failures, Brownie gulped and the bottle was emptied. Brownie recovered, although it remained a question how much medication went inside compared with the considerable portion which covered our hands and spattered our clothing.

Even so, holding a cow's head was far preferable to struggling with a pig. Raising pigs provided a use for the unsalable portion of the dairy operation - skim milk and whey. Mother insisted that their pen be located across the road and down-wind from the house. As hard as father strove to build a hog-proof pen, the snooty rascals would dig beneath the fence until they could achieve freedom. Rounding up the escapee and directing it back to the pen required concerted action by all available family members. The skill displayed by the pig in finding a small hole through which to escape was equalled by its obstinate blindness to an open gate when being driven directly towards it. In the melee, another porker would get free.

In the "American Agriculturalist," father had taken note of an advertisement by a pig breeder in Vermont who sold the Chester White breed. Their advertised fine qualities of growth rate and hardiness caused father to order a pair of this breed. When they arrived at the Railway Express office in Cattaraugus, father took me with him to help load the crate into the trailer. Upon arriving home, we turned them loose in a new pen especially constructed to contain them.

True to the description, they were a thrifty pair - devouring their food with enthusiasm. Without much to occupy their attention, they soon became bored and started to burrow under their new pen until they had created a hole large enough to squeeze through. Straight to the vegetable garden they headed. Grandma spotted their rampage and called for reinforcements. Getting them back in the pen highlighted their obstinacy. Father reinforced the pen and nailed barbed-wire around the bottom perimeter. It was little deterrent, for soon they were loose again.

After successive recaptures, father grumbled: "The ad should have said they were crossed with groundhogs!" Word spread in the neighborhood about the remarkable burrowing ability of the preacher's fancy hogs.

To curb such tranquility-shattering scenes, father decided to "ring" the pigs. Even my kind mother failed to raise her usual objections to any actions inflicting pain. The pigs lost her support on their last foray into her tomatoes and prize dahlias. Saturday morning was designated for the process which consisted of pinching a metal clamp with sharply-pointed ends into the tender snout of the pig. The rings didn't interfere with eating, but discouraged digging which pressed the sharp points into the sensitive portion of the pig's nose.

Special pliers and clips in hand, father climbed into the pig pen. With knowledgeable distaste, I joined him.

"Grab him," father said, pointing to the pig standing in the corner. I missed. Pigs were not designed with convenient hand-holds. Between us, we cornered him, hanging on to his thrashing legs as we pinned him to the ground. Grasping his head, father pinched the ring into his nose.

Blood-curdling squeals rent the air. Anticipating the second insertion, the creature redoubled its efforts to escape further pain. Only one who has been bitten by a pig or kicked by the sharp hooves of swine can appreciate how much I detested this struggle.

"It's in!" father called. "Let him go." Up the pig scrambled, bolting to the far end of the pen.

"Only one more to go," father encouraged me. Disturbed by the uproar made by his companion, ringing the second pig was even more difficult than the first. "Slopping the hogs," a very apt term for feeding them, was pleasant in contrast to "ringing" them. The expedient was effective. From that point on, the pigs stayed in their prescribed enclosure.

Cows usually gravitated to the barn at milking time in anticipation of being relieved of their load of milk. Brownie, our one Brown Swiss, was independent at this point. Instead of coming dociley like the others, she would often turn up missing. Even calling loudly, "Come boss, come boss," had no effect. My lot was to bring her to the barn. In our small pasture of only three or four acres, hiding places for a cow would seem to have been few. But, due to the roughness of the terrain which was bisected by the meandering creek, Brownie held a decided advantage.

Once I located her, the mission was incomplete. Getting her back to the barn was another contest with the stubborn-willed bovine. Sometimes I had her right up to the barn door when she bolted for freedom. Father expressed concern that the excitement so induced inhibited her from "letting her milk down." Of all of the cows we ever owned, she was most adept at putting her foot in the pail or kicking it over when it was almost full. Restraining her tail during milking was often necessary to avoid the deadly accuracy of that flailing whip.

These antics, in conjunction with her low milk output, led father to the unpopular decision that her role would be to provide meat for the winter instead of milk.

Other farm children had horses to ride, albeit plodding draft animals instead of spirited Arabians. Some even had ponies of their own. My deprivation weighed heavily enough on me to drive me to desperate action. Father usually sold for veal the calves born to our cows. On a few occasions he retained an especially fine heifer calf for possible replacement in the dairy herd. At this particular point in time we had one such animal that was about half grown. I decided to try to train her to ride. Prudently I did not share this aspiration with my parents.

This day seemed auspicious for the attempt. Father was away. Both mother and grandmother were busy canning beans.

"Irving," I asked, "Would you come and help me with a project?"

Past experience had made him wary. "Not now," he demurred.

"It won't take long," I promised. He was still reluctant to comply with my request.

"I'll let you use my colored pencils," I promised. For several days he had been begging me to let him borrow them. At that, he consented.

We found the young heifer grazing behind the barn near the straw stack. As I outlined my plan, Irving stared at me.

"After I climb up on the straw stack, all you have to do is to coax the heifer next to the stack. I'll take it from there."

From atop the stack I waited anxiously as Irving pulled a little bunch of alfalfa and edged towards me with the heifer following. It was all going according to plan. At what seemed the opportune moment, I slid down the stack, landing directly on her back.

I was totally unprepared for the next wild moments. They resembled the bucking horse competition at a rodeo except that I had no saddle or bridle to influence the heifer's wild activity. The valley passed in panoramic view as I was catapulted from her back to the ground.

Irving ran over to me. "Arnold, are you hurt?" he demanded.

I lay on the ground, stunned. With the breath knocked out of me, some moments passed before I could respond.

"I'm all right," I feebly reassured him as I staggered clumsily to my feet. Then he helped to brush away some of the barnyard dirt from my soiled clothing. I limped back to the house, dreading mother's reaction.

But she was all caring parent. Her examination revealed no broken bones, although I was bruised and sore for several days. Irving retrieved my glasses, which had been bent double at the nosepiece so one lens was on top of the other.

On the drive to the oculist, I had plenty of time to explain to father what had occurred. Fortunately Dr. Hanvey was able to restore the frames to a reasonable semblance of their former shape. This episode constituted another memorable first and last to my well-remembered experiences in the valley.

"What's For Supper?"

For many, hunger was a characteristic of the Depression years. But, for the parsonage family, this was not the case. My parents' frugality and the diligence with which they gleaned from nature's storehouse made much of the difference.

I knew spring had arrived when Grandma Willis announced: "Let's go and get a mess of cowslips for supper."

Although I didn't care much for these native greens, I did enjoy scouting the backwaters of the creek for these plants with large green leaves and bright yellow flowers. Grandma pointed out the most succulent patches and sent me slogging through the mud to gather enough to fill her dish pan. Marsh Marigold is another name for this earliest of edible plants locally known as cowslips.

Not so enjoyable was Grandma's next project. After a few warm days, she announced: "The horseradish is showing. Arnold, I need your help."

I knew where the patch grew behind the parsonage. With a spade, I dug a bushel basket full of the gnarled roots and washed them thoroughly with water from the pump. When they were clean enough to suit grandma, we went into production out in the yard to keep both the mess and the odor out of the house.

As grandma fed the roots into the old grinder, I turned the handle. The full fury of the irritating substance attacked my mucous membranes. My eyes and nose ran copiously. Grandma believed so fervently in the therapeutic value of fresh horseradish in the spring that my discomfort didn't faze her. I suffered through the grinding process with the hope that some day child labor laws or statutes forbidding cruel and unusual punishments would free me from this horrendous servitude. I could hardly await the day when Irving would be old enough to take my place.

Accumulating food in various forms for the long winter season took many forms. We canned vegetables from the garden except for beets and carrots which were covered with a layer of damp sand in the cellar. Wild strawberries from the fields were so small and time-consuming to fix that immediate consumption was inevitable. The flavor and aroma of their cultivated cousins was bland in contrast. Wild red and black raspberries came early in August, followed closely by the prolific blackberries.

Mother's invitation, "Let's go berrying," brought Irving and me on the run. We led the way over the fence and across the creek to the ascent of the hill behind the parsonage.

Teresa, our three-colored cat, came along on these expeditions even though it meant crossing the creek. Cats usually avoid water. But Teresa was different. If she couldn't find a log or stones to make a dry passage, into the stream she went. On the opposite bank she tried to shake the water out of her fur. Sometimes we took pity on her and carried her across.

Father wouldn't let us keep a dog, but he tolerated a modest supply of cats, so long as it didn't exceed three. He viewed them as the extermination squad to control the mouse and rat population in both house and barn.

Teresa lived a long and fruitful life, dying at the ripe old age of fourteen. We found her curled up in a cradle in the attic, lifelike, but lifeless.

One of Teresa's peculiarities was her insistence on having her batches of kittens in this cradle. She always managed to get there at the auspicious moment. Teresa did more than her normal share of assuring the continuity of the species. Thirteen kittens arrived in one bumper batch. Disposing of them often created tension between my practical father and my tender-hearted mother. Father always solved the problem one way or another, often without mother's knowledge. However, cats did serve as protectors of the harvest.

Logging had opened up areas on the hill where wild berries flourished. In the best patches, filling a milk pail with the shiny juicy fruit was not difficult. Keeping arms and legs covered was only limited protection against their sharp thorns. One merit of blackberries was that they cost nothing but our effort in picking them.

Sometimes we went over west to the Nine Holes area where picking was excellent due to extensive logging. On one expedition to this rather wild tract, we separated in search of the best berries. As I picked on one side of some tall bushes, I heard sounds of trampling on the opposite side. Expecting to find another member of my family, I walked around the clump.

Erect on his hind legs stood a black bear. Into his big red mouth he was stuffing the luscious berries, leaves, twigs, and all. Simultaneously we saw each other. Instantly we both retreated, but in opposite directions.

Running pell-mell in fright, I almost bumped into father. After catching my breath, I gasped, "I just saw a bear." By then others of our party had assembled. "Oh, sure you did," was their skeptical response. Only after bringing them to the spot where the bear tracks still showed in the damp earth could I convince them that my tale was not the product of an overactive imagination. The rest of that afternoon I did not wander far from my group.

We enjoyed blackberries prepared in a number of ways. I ate them fresh on cereal. Mother made them up into pies, cobblers, and various desserts. Canning preserved them for later use. Jelly making was a long and fussy process, but resulted in a form where the seeds were removed.

Except among the Amish, sheaves now have no practical meaning. To me, they were more than an interesting feature of a quaint rural scene. Father always planted some wheat for our own use as chicken feed and breakfast cereal. When the maturing grain turned a golden yellow, father arranged for Albert Pratt, Don's grandfather, to come with his binder to cut the field. The horse-drawn reaper was not far removed from the original machine invented by Cyrus McCormick. As it cut off the grain, a revolving reel knocked the stalks backwards onto a moving belt which carried them up to accumulate into a bundle. When the bundle reached a predetermined size, mechanical fingers tied and ejected it to the side of the reaper.

To avoid wasting some of grain, prior to the machine's first swath around the field, a band of appropriate width was "cradled." The grain was cut with a device which looked like a scythe with a wooden rack attached. These fingers caught and collected the grain into orderly bunches which could be hand-tied into bundles. Manipulating this heavy, cumbersome affair took a sturdy person with real skill. Before the binder became available, the cradle was the normal tool used in reaping entire fields.

Because the reaper was a ponderous machine, often three or four horses were used to pull it instead of just one team. I was fascinated by this mechanical wonder, especially its ability to tie snug knots in the heavy twine.

Freshly cut grain needed to be exposed to the sun so the kernels would dry out before threshing. My assignment was to follow the binder around the field and pick up the bundles, setting them up by pairs, leaned one against the other, in groups of six or eight. The ideal was to do this in a manner resulting in evenly spaced shocks in neat rows, all bundles erect with the heads of grain exposed to the air. My performance seldom reached this standard.

"Fix that shock over there," father admonished, pointing to the offending grain. "It will fall down before we even get out of the field." Off I went to remedy my error.

Even tough jeans didn't thwart the needle-pointed thistles in some bundles as I grabbed them by their strings and held them between my legs to set them in place. By the end of the job, the insides of both legs were sore and irritated. I was glad our field was relatively small.

In those days, before the advent of the combine, when the grain was dry, father and I hauled the bundles from the field on the trailer pulled by the Chevy. We stacked them in a compact pile near the barn in readiness for the day of threshing. Threshing bees were community activities when farmers "changed work" with one another. The stationary threshing machine used in our valley was owned and operated by Martin Westfall. He took his rig from farm to farm, hauling it with a big Case tractor which provided the power to run the separator.

"The threshers will be here Saturday," father announced at supper. This information started a sequence of activities in our kitchen. The term, "to eat like a thresher," was indicative of the huge appetites induced by the vigorous, dirty work. No housewife wanted to be thought lacking in satisfying the hunger of the crew. Roast beef, mashed potatoes, homemade bread, vegetables, and a variety of pies often constituted the menu. Mother and grandma were always equal to this challenge, baking and cooking food in advance on the old wood-burning kitchen range.

"He's coming. He's coming!" I yelled.

Father had appointed me as lookout to warn him when Westfall came into sight. Father directed the placement of the big machine next to our stack. By the time Westfall had leveled the separator and had connected the tractor to it with a wide belt, help had arrived. The roar of the tractor and the deafening din of the machinery drowned out ordinary conversation.

Helpers pitched bundles of wheat onto the feed table at one end and golden grain cascaded out of the delivery chute and into the waiting sacks. I preferred bagging to other tasks, and it was here that father found me. I knew what was coming.

"Son, I need you up on the stack. Here. Take this fork. Keep the stack level. Tramp it down well."

Climbing up on the stack, I was deluged with a steady shower of straw and chaff raining down from the discharge chute on top of the threshing machine. Prickly chaff stuck to my sweat-soaked back and trickled down under my shirt and trousers, filling my socks and shoes. Dust clogged my nose and throat, making breathing difficult. Trying to see what I was doing through the yellow haze was almost impossible, as my glasses collected a coating of dust. Just when I thought I could endure it no longer, a sudden silence signaled release. I slid down the stack,and removed my shirt to dislodge some of the irritating accumulation.

The threshers washed up in big basins of warm water set on potato crates outside the back door. When they gathered around the expanded table inside, there was an abnormal pause before the hungry men filled their plates. Father gave extended and ample thanks for not only the meal, but for the harvest and those who had assisted so ably.

After dinner the whole assemblage moved to an adjacent farm, as our crop was puny in quantity compared with others where threshing took more than one day. As silence descended on the parsonage fields, I headed for the creek to remove the sweaty accumulation of dust and chaff.

The climate of Brooklyn valley was not conducive to fruit growing. Since annual conference was usually held at North Chili, near the Lake Ontario fruit belt, father always planned to bring back peaches and pears which ripened about that time. Removing the back seat from the old Chevy enabled him to crowd in more baskets of fruit than our family needed.

"Pastor. Could you get me a bushel of peaches?" Mildred Bergholtz asked. Others offered their requests. These sales helped defray the expenses of travel.

Father's return from conference launched a frenzy of activities in peeling, processing, and storing the canned fruit. All family members participated.

"Arnold. You've sampled enough," grandma remonstrated. She thought that I was running too many quality checks on the luscious peaches, as I carefully arranged the golden halves in the canning jars. Canned peaches for Sunday evening supper were almost a tradition at our house.

One consequence of having so few farm animals was that each acquired a name and was treated a bit like a member of the family. A problem arose when the time came to convert them into meat. Mother never handled this very well. Instead of a joyous celebration of the laying up of winter supplies, it bore more of the qualities of a funeral. My responses were strongly conditioned by her feelings.

Butchering took place late in the fall when the weather had turned cold, as we had no refrigeration to preserve meat. I recall vividly the fateful day in mid-November when father and Willie Wing led unsuspecting Brownie, the Brown Swiss, from the barn and down behind the Davis barn by the creek. At that moment I would have gladly forgiven Brownie for all of her misdeeds. The sound of a shot which followed soon after seemed to us in the house more like an execution. I saw tears trickle down mother's cheeks as she later placed the cubes of beef in the canning jars for processing. She never ate one bite of that beef.

My Grandmother Willis was made of sturdier stuff. Although a very kind person, enduring the potato famine in Ireland and making her way alone to the United States had given her a practical, no-nonsense approach. When necessity dictated, more than one rooster lost his head at the chopping block as she wielded the ax. Starvation would not have brought mother to take such action.

Even the slaughter of the hogs was traumatic. It was always a bloody affair at which Willie officiated. The squeals of the stuck hogs were ringing in my ears as I was called to assist. I helped in the unpleasant task of removing with hand scrapers the bristles from the skin of the hogs. The freshly killed animals had already been plunged into a huge iron kettle of boiling water heated over an open fire. We canned some of the meat but set aside the hams and bacon for smoking. The process of preserving the hams and bacon involved two stages, the first of which was to immerse them in a brine and chemical solution for a period of weeks.

Next, we removed them from the big earthenware crock for smoking. Father took great care to construct a small wooden enclosure with hooks in the top from which to suspend the meat. A smoky fire of corn cobs and wood, preferably hickory, was periodically renewed over a period of weeks until the outsides of the hams and bacon were a leathery brown and the smoke had permeated and seasoned the meat.

On our way home from church one Sunday, mother cried out: "Elmer. The smokehouse is on fire!"

Bringing the old Chevy to a screeching halt in the yard, father dashed into the shed lean-to, grabbed a pail of water, and doused the blaze. He pulled open the sagging door and picked up two hams which had fallen into the coals when the twine holding them had burned through. Since this had just happened, they were salvaged in the nick of time without significant damage.

Baskets of potatoes which we had raised were piled in one

corner of the damp cellar next to boxes of several varieties of apples. On crude but sturdy shelves mother displayed rows of home-canned vegetables, fruit, and meat. Thus prepared, the parsonage family was ready for winter in Brooklyn valley.

Seeing Eye to Eye With a Wolf

"Yes, I'm getting up," I acknowledged father's call to arise. Gingerly I touched my feet to the cold floor and headed for the area near the stovepipe which provided the skimpy source of heat for the bedroom where my brother and I slept. Since none of the upstairs was heated, warm soapstones wrapped in flannel had tempered the chill of the flannel sheets the night before as I had prepared quickly for bed. Body heat I tried to preserve by hibernating under a mound of home-made quilts with just my eyes and nose exposed to the drafts of the old house. Losing no time in dressing, I was too eager to hurry downstairs by the roaring Round Oak stove to get really warm. I had no premonition that this day would differ substantially from any other winter school day.

Father had arisen earlier to milk the cows and mother hadn't yet come out to prepare breakfast. Dawn was creeping in slowly with the half-light of a gray winter's day making outside objects dimly visible through the heavily frosted panes. While basking in the stove's glow, turning from side to back and around again like a chicken on a vertical spit, I heard a bark followed by a growl. Running to the living room window, I scraped away the frost, blowing on the pane to melt the ice. Peering out, I saw a gray dog on our porch.

Apparently he heard or saw me about that same moment, for he trotted over and placed his big paws on the outside window sill. For what seemed like a very long time, although it probably lasted only a minute or so, I looked into the eyes of this dog as his gleaming pupils stared back. I don't know what was passing through his canine brain, but I was wondering whose dog this was. I was sure I knew every dog in our neighborhood. With just the windowpane between us, his sudden growl, revealing sharp white teeth, startled me. At that moment, mother appeared from her bedroom. As she started breakfast, I told her about the big dog.

In our home, breakfast was never "instant" anything. Father had kindled the fire in the old kitchen range before going to the barn, so the griddles were warming up and the battered teakettle was starting to sing. Breakfast was usually cooked cereal, as eggs could be sold or traded and mother didn't like eggs for breakfast.

The cereal came from the wheat grown on our acres. Father selected some of the best of the crop for home use. Weekly we had a session of "picking over" a batch of wheat kernels, carefully removing bits of dirt, other seeds, and whatever tare had not been separated out in the threshing process. Mother placed the grain in the oven of the old range where the ambient heat from cooking kept it warm, drying out any remaining moisture. I turned the crank of the old coffee mill which cracked the wheat kernels into coarse bits, not fine like ground flour. Mother cooked this cracked wheat cereal for about half an hour, stirring it frequently to prevent lumping and sticking on the bottom of the pan. I topped it with maple syrup or sugar, as we seldom could afford cane sugar. Surrounded by a moat of milk in the bowl, it was sturdy stuff!

"Watch for father to come from the barn," mother requested. She wanted to finish up breakfast preparation by making toast out of home-made bread. She placed the thick slices on a wire rack above the coals after removing one griddle. Served with butter, soft maple sugar, or some of grandma's blackberry jelly, it went well with the cereal.

Watching for father, I noticed the dog scratching at the outer barn door, which would usually have been ajar. As the door opened slowly, father appeared, wielding the pitchfork defensively with one hand as he carried the pail of milk in the other. Avoiding the sharp tines, the dog retreated a safe distance as father crossed the road and reached the protection of the woodshed door at the back of the house. Removing his outside barn clothes in the woodshed, father washed up at the old wooden sink. He used a dipper of warm water from the tank on one end of the kitchen range. Grandma Willis and my brother Irving had appeared, so we all sat down together for breakfast.

After father offered the blessing, he quickly recited the unusual events of the morning.

"I was walking across to the barn, milk pail in one hand and the lighted buggy lantern with the big red bull's-eye in the other, when the milk truck came along. In the light of the truck's headlights, I saw a big gray dog racing with the truck down the snow-covered road. As soon as the truck had passed, I started to cross the road. Suddenly the dog returned from following the truck. Growling in an unfriendly manner, the dog darted towards me. I swung the lantern at the beast. The flame of the wick and the ruby glow of the bull's-eye lens temporarily frightened him. I hurried into the barn, taking care to drop the latch on the outside door."

"What happened then?" we chorused as if on cue.

"All the time I was feeding the cows, milking, and doing the other chores, I heard it whining and trying with his paws to pull open the door. Since it had gotten lighter, I thought the pitchfork would give better protection than the lantern. I jabbed at his nose. He ran over in the garden and I went to the house."

The topic made breakfast table conversation more animated than usual. "Do you think he's someone's dog?" I asked.

"At first I thought he belonged to the truck driver," father replied. "I suspected the driver had let him run for some exercise from one pickup dock to the next. But now I don't believe that's the case. I wonder if it isn't a wolf."

Then mother contributed: "Last week the mailman told me that his horse had shied and panicked on his route over by Mock Hill." In the winter, Adolph Meyer often delivered mail with a horse-drawn pung or cutter which enabled him to take to the fields when roads were drifted. Previously his horse had run away, overturning the sleigh near Gene Wing's farm. In this incident, the harness had been torn up and Adolph had been injured.

Then I recalled, "Lillian Woodard told me that Day Booth had been helping them butcher hogs. While he was walking home crosslots, a big gray dog started to circle him. He threw sticks at it but it followed him all the way home. Only then did he realize that the blood on his hands had gotten on the sticks and excited the beast." I reinforced this account by telling how the three Woodard children had also been circled by a gray dog while on their way to school.

Up until now, these reports had been highly discounted as overactive imagination. But others had reported seeing a gray beast slinking into the woods or having farm animals stampede in fear. Suddenly, around our breakfast table, these stories took on an aura of credibility.

Father always liked to sit where he could see any traffic on the road, although on our stretch it was usually sparse. Suddenly, right in the middle of breakfast, he pushed back his chair, explaining, "I think Raymond Oakes is going by." Out the front door he hurried, not stopping for wraps. Raymond was a local trapper who was on his way to check traps.

Eager to learn what was happening, I stepped outside where I heard father describing the events of the morning. Father pointed out the gray dog, which by this time was nosing around Charles Wing's house next door.

"He's alone, old, and quite feeble," father noted of his neighbor. "I think that thing is a threat to him and to the entire community."

"I agree," Raymond concurred. "Hold my dogs while I take care of him." While father held the leashes of Raymond's two hounds who were yelping and jerking in excitement, Raymond approached the beast and put two bullets through his head.

"I'll be back to pick it up after checking traps," Raymond promised as he retrieved his hounds and went whistling down the road.

All of the above had consumed so much time that I was in danger of being tardy for school. Then two remarkable departures from normal routine took place. I could scarcely believe my ears!

Glancing at the clock, father declared, "I don't think we have time for family devotions this morning."

Mother followed up in a tone I rarely heard her use: "Elmer. Take Arnold to school with the car. It just isn't safe to have him walking with animals like that on the loose." It was a declaration and not a request. After token resistance, father agreed.

This was not the simple process of jumping into the car, hitting the starter, and taking off. If the old '28 Chevy had any redeeming qualities, starting easily in winter was not one of them. In cold weather the engine could not be coaxed into life without a series of actions calculated to provide assistance and support to the old "bucket of bolts." Required was a full pail of hot water to be ladled over the manifold and other portions of the engine, removing the chill from its iron bones.

Mother was called to assist by engaging the starter while father simultaneously turned the crank or tinkered under the hood with the choke or gas controls. If fortune smiled, there would be sound, a puff of smoke, and a reducing noise level as oil reached the bearings. Father would urge mother to keep pumping the accelerator, lest life suddenly depart and the process have to be repeated. Often a second or third attempt failed as the cold battery expired and turning on the ignition provoked only a sick hum or click of the solenoid.

In case of true emergency, one more expedient was attempted. All of the family, including grandma, would be called to push the reluctant vehicle out of the barn and onto the highway, the front end of the car pointing down the small grade towards Brooklyn bridge. With mother at the wheel (about the only time she ever drove), the rest of the family pushed with might and main to gain as much momentum as possible. At this moment, father would yell, "Now, Eva," and mother would pop the clutch. More than half of the time failure would strike, and mother would steer the car to the side of the road to await a tow from a passing neighbor.

This morning the fates were favorable. Due to the low temperatures, father had covered the hood with a heavy horse blanket the night before after he had returned from town. Plenty of hot water was available, and the Chevy was in a good mood. Even so, I was late to school. Father went to the door with me and explained to the teacher the reason for my tardiness.

In a way, I held a bit of celebrity status the rest of the day. "Tell us all about it," the students demanded at recess. Even the teacher listened in. At noon hour I answered more questions as rumors of previous encounters were re-hashed. In spite of this, the day dragged, as I was anxious to see the dead wolf.

On my way home, I stopped at Willie Wing's shanty where he and Raymond stayed. Raymond was finishing the process of skinning the beast when I arrived. How different it looked in this gory state from the way he had appeared as I had stared him in the eye that morning, separated by a single pane of glass. I experienced a mixture of relief and sadness, as I never wanted a part in killing anything.

On advice of the local game warden, Raymond surrendered the head and the pelt to be shipped to the state conservation office in Albany for verification. In due time word came back to silence the scoffers who had belittled the event. Indeed it was a Canadian timber wolf which had probably come across Lake Erie on the ice and met his fate in Brooklyn valley.

For three days mother had her way and I was chauffeured to school by a reluctant father. Eventually even mother agreed that since the wolf was dead and nothing more was heard of sightings in our area that continuing the practice was no longer necessary. I resumed the daily trudge to and from school and thought about the futility of driving a boy to school AFTER the wolf was dead.

Snakes, Wasps, and Other Sunday Distractions

The little white church with the rounded steeple was fully as central in the lives of the inhabitants of the valley as it was in their physical view. Occupying a commanding location at the T in the road, it could be seen for some distance directly ahead by those traveling west on the Brooklyn highway. In those days it was strikingly framed by four huge elm trees which arched gracefully above it. The slim, pendulous extremities of their branches formed preferred nesting places for Baltimore Orioles. In front of the trees and just behind the edifice stretched the church sheds, open stalls facing east towards the road to protect the parishioners' horses from the prevailing westerly winds and winter snows. The ubiquitous privy stood alone at the north end of the sheds, in plain view of the worshippers in the church. From one arm of the T, the road led over Hammond Hill, down into Zoar Valley, and up again to Springville, the destination for serious shopping. The other arm wound up the grade and through a hollow in the hills to East Otto, just three miles distant.

The rectangular frame structure, covered with clapboards painted white, was rescued from uninteresting plainness by two features. The first was the cupola-like steeple and the second the arced front door and windows with their forest green shutters. Father believed in informing the public about the times for services. He purchased a kit and fashioned a glass-covered bulletin board mounted to the left of the front door. Its moveable letters and numbers permitted keeping the information current. The great brass key to the lock in the front door was kept in a crevice behind the sign. Although the church was locked when not in use, almost everyone in the community knew where the key was secreted.

Abutting the front of the church, a concrete slab stretching the width of the building provided a dry area where worshipers could clean the mud from their footwear. Over the years, settling and frost had fractured this slab, creating several crevices of up to two inches in width. In spring or summer the moment I arrived at church, I hurried over to examine the contents of these cracks.

"Irving, come look at this," I called. Two colorful garter snakes, yellow with black markings, were stretched out in one of the breaks in the concrete, sunning themselves.

"I've found a snake skin," Irving exclaimed. "I'm going to save it."

"Look at this big one. He's feisty," I poked it with a stick and it fled for refuge under a rock.

"Come on inside. It's time for Sunday School," father interrupted our quest. Apparently he was unaware that our thoughts would not accompany our bodies to class.

The church had no basement, but rested on a stone foundation laid up dry-wall fashion without mortar between the stones. In my boyish imagination, I conjured up scenes of writhing masses of serpents beneath the entire structure.

The inside of the church was plain, with the exception of the window tops and a metal covering of the ceiling which had been embossed with a pattern that repeated regularly throughout its expanse. The intrusion of the entry-way with its swinging door opening into the sanctuary left a small area at each side used for Sunday School classes. In the center of each of these recesses stood a black cast-iron stove about five feet long and two feet wide. The shuttered door at one end of each stove opened to accommodate logs three feet or more in length. Emerging from the opposite end, the black stove pipe rose and then wandered in several ninety-degree angles to connect with the chimney. The theory behind this circuitous route was that the long pipes squeezed the maximum amount of heat from the exhausted air before it was discharged into the outside atmosphere.

Plain wooden benches with backs boasted no adornment and clearly proclaimed their source as ordinary boards. Utility rather than comfort was the goal of their builder, so occupiers of these pews were not encouraged to slumber. A small raised platform bordered by an altar rail set off the pulpit and three chairs. On either side of this platform, occupying about the same areas as the recesses at the rear, two short pews faced the pulpit. These were referred to as the "Amen corners."

When father returned to Brooklyn in 1929, the illumination for evening services came from six oil lamps in swinging cast iron brackets spaced along the sides plus a large chandelier above the center aisle holding eight or ten lamps. At best, the light cast by this collection of lamps was barely sufficient for the congregation to read the hymn books.

Saturday morning father reminded me, "The lamps at church need attention. Be sure to trim the wicks."

"But I was going to play with Don this morning," I protested.

"Take care of your jobs first and then go," was his solution.

At church, I took down all of these lamps, filled them with kerosene oil from a five-gallon can, and trimmed the wicks. With great care I polished the delicate chimneys inside and out, removing the black residue from the glass. After replacing them in their brackets with wicks turned to cast maximum light, I joined Don, who was waiting for me.

Looking back, I now realize that my distaste for this chore came from its dirtiness. My hands were always smudged with the black and were oily and reeked with the odor of kerosene. With no facilities to do so at church, washing my hands had to wait until I reached home. The pungent odor of kerosene persisted even after thorough washing with soap and water. I reminded myself that the quality of my performance went on display weekly for all to see.

In 1934 an entirely new light was cast on this dim scene. Somewhere father obtained two old Coleman gasoline lanterns. After replacement of generators, mantles, and globes, these devices were welcome substitutes for the oil lamps.

"Father, I'd like to help," I suggested. The novelty of the new lights interested me.

To my surprise, he turned down my offer. "The mantles are very fragile," he explained. "And gasoline is much more dangerous than kerosene. I don't want an explosion." Progress had freed me from one despised job.

On the first Sunday after the new lights were obtained, a larger than normal congregation turned out for evening service. Following the usual song time and preliminaries, father launched into his sermon. Father's sermons were never brief, not even at night. Gradually but perceptibly the white light became dimmer and more yellow. How long the Coleman lanterns would burn was limited more by the compressed air supply than the capacity of the fuel tank. With the air supply running low, I hoped sacrilegiously that father would take the hint and terminate his message.

These unfounded hopes were quickly dashed, as father grabbed a chair from the pulpit and reached up to lift each lantern down from its iron hook. Placing them on the front seat, he pumped up the pressure until the white light again starkly illuminated the room. Replacing the lanterns on their hooks suspended from the ceiling, he resumed his sermon with no break in his train of thought.

In the Spring of 1936, the Brooklyn Free Methodist Church celebrated the 75th anniversary of its founding. A highlight of that occasion was the taking of pledges for the purchase of electric light fixtures for the church. Electric lines were being strung in the valley, making oil and gasoline lights only a distant memory.

One wintry Sunday evening, after the service had concluded, father suggested: "Eva, I need to talk with someone. Why don't the rest of you go on home instead of waiting?"

Because of the cold, we had walked to church instead of going through the hassle of starting the car. Grandma, mother, and I had been home about half an hour before father arrived, weary after three services plus chores. He had just settled down in the rocking chair with his feet on the stove when mother suddenly demanded: "Where is Irving?"

"Didn't you bring him?" father asked incredulously.

"No. He was asleep on the seat and I thought you'd carry him when you came. At four years old, he's so heavy to lug."

Grandma got into the act. "Elmer, get right back to church. Suppose he wakes up and finds himself all alone in the dark? That would be terrible."

Pulling on his heavy coat, father relit the lantern and hurried back the half-mile to the darkened church. Still sound asleep, Irving didn't awaken until the nippy outside air hit his face. From that moment on, grandma took it upon herself to make sure that this didn't recur.

On one hot humid Sunday morning I wasn't following the points of father's sermon very closely. The panes of glass in the window near our pew boasted a multitude of imperfections. Bubbles and thicker ridges grotesquely distorted reality. I discovered that with slight movements of my head I could make objects appear as if seen in a trick mirror.

The building seemed to attract wasps and flies, some of them the huge horseflies as well as the common varieties. I watched in fascination as a horsefly landed on Luther Flood's collar, explored his ear, and climbed to the summit of his sweaty bald head. Packing a mean bite, the horsefly nipped the drowsing farmer. Jerking awake, Brother Flood slapped his head with his calloused hand. He missed. The fly buzzed off to safety on the ceiling.

My attention then was diverted to the action in the pew just in front of us. An aggressive wasp had singled out Lucile Fleckenstein for dive bombing practice. On each pass, she ducked away as she heard him coming. The wasp miscalculated when she jerked her head sideways and the insect became entangled in her long brown hair. Grandma, sitting directly behind Lucile, swatted the wasp with her Sunday School quarterly. I watched it drop to the floor where grandma stepped on it. The next thing I knew, everyone was standing for the doxology. I readied myself for a quick exit to see how the snakes were doing.

In the winter, the fire in the stove had to be started on Sunday morning and Wednesday night. If the parsonage had been adjacent to the church, this duty would have been much easier. Instead, each trip to build the fire or check on the stove required a round trip of one mile. Even though the fire apparently was in a healthy state of combustion when I left it, on my return it might either have expired or be roaring furiously, turning the stove pipe a cherry red. The old stove was temperamental, seeming to take delight in performing the unexpected. Father never fully trusted my judgment in tending this fire, as the comfort of the congregation depended on its whims. In cold weather, the pastor might look out on his congregation bundled up in winter coats or mopping their brows while fanning away with a Sunday School paper.

My memories of church are etched clearly because of the time I spent in the various services. On a typical Sabbath, Sunday School started at ten, followed by morning worship at eleven. At noon occurred a traditional Methodist activity - the class meeting. Elbert Harrison, a tall, spare bachelor, functioned as the class leader. During the session he inquired specifically into the spiritual state of each person present. I found this to be uncomfortable at times, and envied the other children, most of whom left at the close of the morning service.

Usually father managed to hold a Sunday afternoon service somewhere in the area. This often included Sunday School. Chores had to be done in between this and the evening service at seven-thirty, preceded by young people's service at seven. On many Sundays I spent six or seven hours in services.

Father's outreach into neighboring areas disclosed small settlements where the inhabitants had no contact with church. He earnestly tried to fill this void. While at Brooklyn, one secondary location for his efforts was Ashford Hollow, a spot known for the outlawed dispensing of alcoholic beverages, for these were Prohibition days.

He located a little one-room country schoolhouse on top of the steep ridge between Ashford Hollow and West Valley. The main families I recall were the Macks, with ten red-headed children, the Wheelers, and a couple who eked out a living by collecting eggs from farmers and reselling them at the Farmers Market on Broadway Avenue in Buffalo. No one even thought of raising the question of separation of church and state because of using the schoolhouse. Instead, people were pleased that anyone would show interest in the lives of these children and their parents, so impoverished physically, mentally, and spiritually.

Although a Methodist Episcopal Church was active at East Otto village, the people father contacted were mainly unchurched and did not feel comfortable attending that place of worship. In reality, no significant sense of competition developed, as farm families in the valley considered the white church at the crossroads to be their church, whether or not they attended regularly. Consequently father was viewed as their parson to be called upon for weddings, funerals, or when illness struck. So, in more than one sense, the church functioned as a focal point in the life of the valley.

From Weddings to Funerals

A timid knock on our front door roused father from his Saturday night sermon preparation. An obviously nervous young man and woman appeared in the lamplight.

"Will you marry us?" the young man inquired.

"Come in and we'll talk about it," father offered.

Carrying out the functions of a pastor to a small rural community involved father in the lives of the people at times of joy and sorrow, crisis and celebration. As the only resident clergyman in the immediate area, he received more than the average number of calls for such occasions.

Some of the happy times were in connection with weddings - not usually the formal church ceremony variety, but more often officiating at the simple exchanging of vows in the living room of the parsonage. For some reason, the time most frequently selected by the participants was Saturday evening, when, following chores, father was working on his sermons for Sunday. Since we had no telephone, they couldn't just call up. Often the ink on the marriage license was still damp as they had come directly from the town clerk's house. Although father never solicited this business, I'm sure that the town clerk sometimes made suggestions and provided specific directions for reaching the Brooklyn parsonage.

To meet legal requirements, the marriage ceremony had to be witnessed by two adults. Providing for this formality sometimes never entered the heads of some prospective brides and grooms. To make up for this oversight, mother and Grandma Willis graciously filled that role even when this meant getting dressed again after having retired for the night.

Seldom did the bride have flowers. In summertime mother picked a bridal bouquet from her own flower garden while the participants waited. Although the clothing the couple wore was doubtless their best, this didn't necessarily mean a suit and a long gown.

Father never simply performed the marriage ceremony. First, he talked with the couple at some length, seeking to find out their background and the degree of their commitment to one another. Only after impressing them with the seriousness of the step they were contemplating did he proceed with the ceremony. While in no way condoning their obvious tardiness in formalizing their relationship, father solemnized the vows for several couples in the presence of one or more of their joint offspring. His theory was "Better late than never."

Honorariums he received for performing weddings ranged from nothing to a high of five dollars. Father always presented to each couple an attractive white book, "Our Wedding," containing the official certificate plus space for other appropriate entries to commemorate the event. On the average, the money he received barely covered his cost of this book of remembrance.

Some fifty years after tieing the knot for one couple, they appeared at the door of his home on Jefferson Street in Cattaraugus where he and mother had chosen to retire. The purpose of this visit was to present father and mother with a sizable check in expression of their appreciation. Their marriage had endured half a century and they had prospered in farming. Now they wanted to do something to make up for the fee which they now felt had been inadequate. The sentiment meant even more to my parents than the amount of the check.

Although father was a student of the Bible and never shirked in his faithful sermon preparation, he probably wasn't remembered primarily as a great preacher. Instead, his strength as a pastor lay in his concern for people. Foremost in his mind was their spiritual welfare. He was usually quite direct about this, inquiring, "Brother X, how is it with your soul today?" Although this made a few people feel uncomfortable, they recognized the sincerity of his concern.

In spite of all of the necessary farm work, father kept a careful record of his extensive visitation. In his "Pastoral Record" books, I found he had often made twenty to thirty calls per week. The Chevy stopped at practically every home within a radius of ten miles. He followed up on couples he had married. Newcomers to the community he welcomed and invited to church. It was not practical to follow current protocol and telephone to arrange for a convenient time. The parsonage had no phone; neither did the majority of these rural homes.

Almost universal was the genuine welcome with which people responded to pastoral calls. My parents encouraged me to come along to make the acquaintance of children at the homes they visited. I was shy and afraid of the strange dogs.

"Please let me stay in the car. I brought along a book to read," I pleaded.

"No," father insisted. "They have a boy and girl about your age."

When our arrival came at all close to mealtime, the farm family often invited us to join them. This friendly practice sounded the death knell for a number of roosters who were sacrificed on the chopping block. It has been said that, of all birds, this fowl is probably the most religious because so many of their number entered the ministry.

Illnesses which today are routinely treated were often fatal in those times. The doctor's best efforts sometimes were of no avail, although his dedication and faithfulness were unquestioned. During the winters of 1934 and 1935 many people succumbed to pneumonia. My brother, Irving, who had narrowly survived scarlet fever our last year in Cattaraugus, seemed susceptible to whatever illness came along.

Arriving home from school one February day in 1935, I saw Dr. Tuttle's black Buick in our driveway. At the wheel was a young man whom the elderly doctor had hired to chauffeur him on his house calls in wintry weather.

Having just come out of my brother's sickroom, the doctor spoke kindly but seriously: "Reverend, you have a very sick boy. It's pneumonia in both lungs. I'll be back to see him tomorrow."

Although it was a twelve-mile trip each way from Cattaraugus, Dr. Tuttle called at the parsonage daily on his rounds over the next two weeks. My mind struggled with the question I dared ask no one: "Is my little brother going to die?"

Then came the day when Dr. Tuttle announced to my parents: "The grip on the boy is broken. He's on the mend. I won't need to stop by tomorrow." I felt a great load lift from my mind.

Dr. Tuttle charged my parents nothing for all of his medical services. His reputation as a crusty character given to profanity hadn't affected father's vision of a needy individual to whom he should witness. A special relationship was forged between the physician and the country parson which remained firm right up to the time of the doctor's death.

The outcomes for others were not always so fortunate. Messages came to the parsonage by night as well as by day that someone was critically ill and wanted the pastor. Whatever he was doing, father responded to all requests. On January 17, 1935, Mrs. Flood stopped at the parsonage on an urgent mission. Father had just come in from evening chores.

"Pastor," she reported, "I don't think Frank Reed will make it through the night. I saw him and his fingernails are starting to turn blue."

Although father had called at the Reed home the day before, he quickly changed his clothes and departed. The pall of gloom hung heavy in our home that evening as we hoped the information was faulty. When father returned, his face revealed the truth. Just over a year later Frank's wife Catherine also died of pneumonia. Their three little blond girls were left parentless: Minnie, age twelve; Phyllis, age eight; and Esther, age six. Their maternal grandparents, the Alfred Wings, took over the responsibility of bringing them up.

I knew them well, especially Minnie, as they attended church and Sunday School at Brooklyn. Even though I very much wanted to extend my sympathy, I just didn't know how to express it.

Funerals were another of the sacraments of the church. These last rites for people he knew so well were always difficult for father, as he endeavored to bring comfort to the bereaved. Here, too, he didn't offer a minimum of liturgy and platitudes. Instead he used these moments to comfort the sorrowing and sound a warning to the unconverted.

I didn't like funerals, and, mercifully, I was usually permitted to stay at home with my grandmother. Father's honoraria on these occasions followed much the same range as for weddings. Weismantel Brothers, Springville morticians, occasionally called on father when the deceased had no family or church affiliation. He never took these assignments lightly.

Near the close of the school year in June 1931 father had received an early morning caller, a not uncommon happening. At school, the normal boisterousness was lacking on the playground. It was there that I learned that Genevieve Steinbar, mother of Preston and Carol, our classmates, had been found unconscious. For several days she lay in a coma produced by an overdose of medication for a chronic illness. The suspense as she lingered between life and death hung heavy throughout the community. A few days later she died, without regaining consciousness. This traumatic event raised some questions in my eight-year-old mind about God and death, especially the "why."

The spring of 1935 was an especially difficult one in the Pratt/Sprowl household as evidenced by the following newspaper accounts which appeared in February in "The Cattaraugus Times":

> Several weeks ago Albert Pratt fell and injured one shoulder. On Saturday night Dr. T. L. Holman lanced an abscess on his ear. About two weeks ago his granddaughter, May Sprowl, contracted bronchial pneumonia and had to be taken to the Mountain Clinic in Olean Monday night, February 17, accompanied by her parents, Mr. and Mrs. Lloyd Sprowl and by Elmer Fleckenstein, Cattaraugus. On Tuesday Mr. Sprowl motored to Bradford and returned to East Otto with Mrs. Viola Glow who expected to help the family. She soon

was in bed with pneumonia on one lung. Mrs. Pratt had been a sufferer for some time with knee trouble and walks with a crutch part of the time. At the clinic little May received oxygen and Mr. Sprowl and Donald traveled to Olean again and found her much improved. Mrs. Steve Ditcher is helping care for the sick at the family home.

* * * * *

Lloyd Sprowl was in Olean Sunday afternoon. Mrs. Viola Glow, who lay in a coma several days this past week, is reported improving. Donald Sprowl was found to be running a high temperature and was taken to the clinic Saturday. Here a spot on one lung was discovered. The same day, Mrs. Lydia Ditcher, who had been helping at the Pratt home caring for the invalids, was found to have contracted pneumonia and was taken to the Townsend Hospital in Gowanda by Dr. E. E. Heier, Cattaraugus. Dr. T. J. Holman, who had been attending physician at the Pratts, had been taken by a malady, announced by some as pneumonia, had been forced to transfer the cases to Dr. Gray of Springville. Mrs. Reuben Higbee of Leon has come to help out the Pratts.

The parsonage family was not immune to sorrow. During breakfast on the morning of May 27, 1932, Albert Pratt appeared at the door to tell us that a telephone call had come for father and that he was to call back. Father accompanied him home to return the call, as this was the nearest telephone in the area.

Good news never seemed to arrive in the form of long-distance phone calls. It wasn't until I returned home from school that afternoon that I learned the substance of the call. Father's only brother, Sidney, just twenty-two years old, had been killed while working at the site where Attica Prison was being built. Father had departed for Elba that morning, leaving mother to look after chores and other duties in his absence. After three long, sad days father returned. From that point in his ministry, he displayed an enhanced ability to empathize with those who lost family members.

Pondering why some lived and others died was not a topic I ever discussed with anyone. However, the death of my uncle and my being made repeatedly aware of the ebb and flow of life in the community forced me to serious contemplation.

Folk remedies were then relied upon for a number of conditions which today would call for the services of medical practitioners. One day my friend, Don Sprowl, and I were climbing around in the loft of a shed which housed the pigs at the Pratt farm. I was wearing the usual knee-high rubber boots appropriate for the stable.

In the dim light, I stepped on a rusty spike jutting out of a board in the floor. In shock and pain I yelled, "Don, help me."

Don hurried over to look. "Don't move," he cautioned.

The spike had penetrated the sole of the boot and pierced the fore part of my foot, exiting through the top of the boot. The pain was excruciating.

Taking charge, Don cautioned: "I'll stand on the board to hold it steady. Then jerk your foot straight up."

Anything seemed better than standing there impaled. Gritting my teeth, I did as he suggested. Now free from the spike, I felt blood oozing into my sock.

"Let's go to the house," he urged.

I worked my way painfully down the cleats which served as a ladder and hobbled over to the house.

"What happened?" Don's mother demanded.

As soon as the facts tumbled out, Don's Grandma Pratt took charge. "Don, bring me an old sap bucket. Lulu, put some ashes in the bottom of it. Shovel some red hot coals from the kitchen range over the bed of ashes."

By then she had seated me on a chair in the old kitchen and had removed my boot and bloody sock. After cleaning off the puncture holes which were still bleeding, she examined my foot.

"Lulu, mix up a cup of salt, a half-cup of brown sugar, and two table-spoons of mustard," she prescribed. "Don. Fetch me a feed bag."

With all in readiness, she poured the odd mixture over the hot coals. "Hold his foot steady, high enough so it won't be burned," Grandma Pratt cautioned. Quickly she packed the feed bag around my leg to contain the smoky incense which had started to ascend.

I suffered both physically and mentally as my leg was held immobile over the smoky bucket for half an hour. My foot felt like a ham in a smokehouse.

"That's enough," Grandma Pratt concluded.

My foot and lower leg emerged, stained a yellow-brown and giving off an aroma like cured meat. To my surprise, much of the soreness was gone. The wound healed cleanly without infection even more rapidly than my foot returned to normal color. All of this took place without benefit of a tetanus shot.

At some point in this whole process, I heard someone utter the dreaded word "lockjaw." Until the wound healed, I lived in terror lest that frightful fate befall me. The fear of illness and death was not a torment reserved only for adults in the valley.

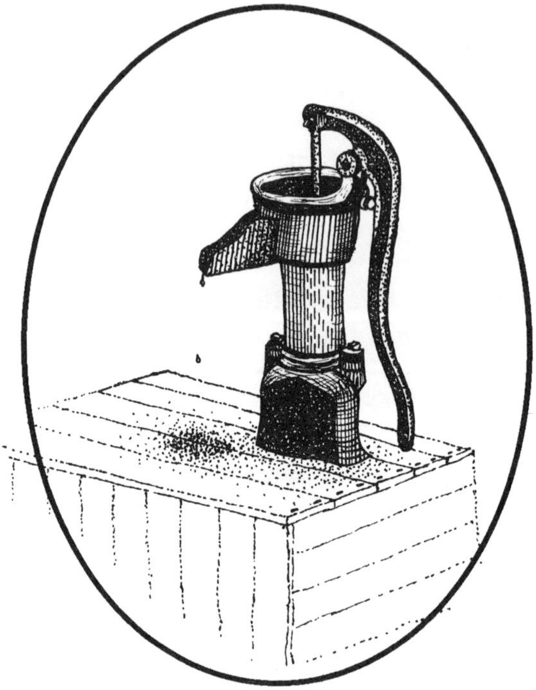

Bootstrap Utilities: Do It Yourself

"Arnold, the water pail is dry!" "Arnold, the wood box is empty!" "Arnold, the living room lamp is out of oil!"

Brooklyn Valley's skyline was devoid of visual clutter. The reason lay not with buried utility lines as in modern high class subdivisions. We simply had no public utilities and had to provide our own substitutes. For the parsonage family, I was intimately involved in the processes of obtaining them.

Furnishing ample liquid for the many essential uses of our household was mainly my responsibility. The source was a pitcher pump located in the woodshed just outside the kitchen door. That it was "indoors" was a decided plus. This pump often "lost its prime." Pouring a small amount of water into the pump was necessary before it could produce enough suction to lift water from the well. The rule was to always reserve enough water to prime the pump. The pump handle and I were close associates but not fast friends. Invariably it seemed that as soon as I settled down to read a book or play a game, the call would come: "Arnold, we're out of water."

Somehow I was expected to anticipate the needs of family and stock. Certain requirements were predictable. Keeping the drinking water pail filled had high priority. It stood on a platform next to the cast iron sink. Just above it on a nail hung a tin dipper. That same dipper touched the lips of all in the household as well as guests. Drawn from a gravel stratum which was spring-fed, the water was sweet and cold when recently pumped.

Second on the list of priorities was filling the tank on the kitchen range where water was heated by the wood fire. When empty, it took three brimming pails to refill. Only on baking days in winter did this supply become really hot. The family used warm water from this reservoir for washing dishes and personal care. Two large teakettles squatting on the back of the stove acted as normal reserves. Twice daily these were heated to boiling and mother used the water to scald the tank, disks, and spouts of our De Laval cream separator.

The chicken drinking troughs needed daily attention. The silly birds lacked enough self-interest to avoid scratching litter into the water trough. Sometimes they tipped it over, permitting the water to gush out. In winter, when not free to drink from the creek, the cows seemed to have an insatiable thirst. The pigs, too, required their share of this essential fluid.

"Remember tomorrow is wash day," mother reminded me on Sunday evening. Father set the Big Ben alarm clock, the only one we owned, to herald the earlier arising time. Responding to its raucous bell, I set about my pre-breakfast task of pumping water to fill the various containers associated with doing the laundry.

The first of these was a large-capacity copper boiler of ancient vintage, its age attested to by multiple soldered patches. I placed it on the kitchen range before filling it. Except in the coldest winter weather, the washing took place in the woodshed where I set up the wooden racks to hold the two washtubs, large round containers with wooden handles. The first one, the wash tub, I filled with hot water from the boiler. The second, the rinse tub, I filled with cold water.

Mother used two instruments for torturing the clothes. She first scrubbed them in soapy water, working them by hand up and down the grooved surface of the washboard. The second tool was a conical metal plunger with a wooden handle. This she vigorously thrust up and down on the clothes in the soapy tub. When I was not at school, I provided the muscle power to turn the crank of the hand wringer which squeezed the water from the washed clothes as mother fed them through the hard rubber rollers. From the wringer, they fell into the rinse tub for more pummeling with the metal dasher to remove the soapy residue. They made a second trip through the ringer to remove as much of the water as possible. Then mother hung them to dry on the clotheslines which were strung between the corner of the house and the maple tree. At this point in the process, if I were home, I promptly emptied the tubs, pailful after pailful, carrying it out to put on the garden. On school days the job was often waiting for me when I returned home.

Drying clothes in the winter was no fun. In zero weather they would start to freeze before mother could pin them to the line. Freeze-dried foods were unheard of but freeze-dried clothes were all too familiar. The stiff forms of long johns and overalls mother carried into the house like cordwood. Inside, they collapsed limply over the wooden drying bars set up around the Round Oak heater in the living room. Red, chapped hands painful with arthritis were part of mother's cost of doing laundry. In the summertime, when I heard the putt-putt of the gasoline-powered Maytag washer at work over at the Pratt farm, I wondered if mother would ever have laundry day that easy.

Saturday night was dedicated to washing different subject matter, for it was bath night. The stove tank, teakettles, and boiler I had to fill in preparation for this ceremony. Mother carried one of the washtubs into the living room, positioning it near the stove. For privacy of a sort, mother pulled down the shades in the living room. Into the tub, I poured a mixture of warm water from the tank on the stove, tempering it with cold water to make it bearable. The Saturday evening bath was a ritual performed in sequential order of age for my brother and me.

"Irving," mother called. "Off with your clothes and into the tub."

"Why can't Arnold go first this time?" he pouted.

"Because he's older," was mother's standard reply.

No one lingered long in the bath, as one side of the body baked while the drafts from the windows quickly chilled the wet flesh on the side opposite the stove. Mother's careful inspection of the completed job sometimes resulted in selective redo of neglected areas.

On one memorable evening Irving had convinced mother that he could "do it by myself." Irving's scream brought the whole family to the living room. He stood in the tub, bare and dripping. Across his buttocks a red line began to glow. In a moment of carelessness the stove had branded him. This reminder of his inattention came painfully to his consciousness for the next days whenever he sat down.

Drying off quickly with the scratchy towels, we donned our nightclothes and scampered up the stairs to bed. This was one time father emptied the tub.

In the summer I pleaded with mother, "I went swimming in the creek this afternoon. I don't need a bath."

"Take your bath," she insisted. "Splashing in the creek is not an equivalent substitute for a proper Saturday night bath."

The only waste water that didn't have to be carried out was that which emptied from the kitchen sink drain through a lead pipe and flowed out on the ground in back of the house. The heat of summer caused an unpleasant odor to develop in this perpetually wet spot. Grandma planted flowers which prospered luxuriantly on the nutrients and constant moisture. Hollyhocks, cosmos, zinnias, and cockscomb made a colorful hedge beautifying this problem area.

During all of this pumping and carrying of water, my mind puzzled over the aquatic marvels up in Bowen Hollow. The Bowen family had installed an amazing device called a hydraulic ram which forced the flow from springs in the valley below their farm uphill to a tank in their attic. I didn't understand how this was accomplished without a pump or motor of any kind, but the idea of running water with no seeming effort strongly appealed to me.

"Father, we have a spring in our pasture. Why can't we fix it up to have running water like the Bowens?" I inquired.

"Son, that would take a lot of money for the pipe, tank, and other equipment. We just can't afford it," was his logical explanation. Even so, I continued to dream.

Our primary source of heat energy was wood because it was readily available and cost little except labor. During the summer father engaged George Fleckenstein to haul in limbs and portions of tree trunks on afternoons when he had completed his milk route. After saw logs had been removed, the loggers were glad to have anyone take away the limbs and imperfect trunks that had been discarded. George Fleckenstein charged father only two dollars per truckload, not covering much more than the cost of gasoline. The pile in our yard grew until father thought it sufficient to last for the heating season.

At breakfast one Friday morning in early October, father announced: "Tomorrow is the buzz bee. I have a crew lined up." I knew he had planned it for Saturday so I could help.

Ward Bergholtz maneuvered Gene Wing's Fordson tractor into position and attached the big drive belt connecting the saw to the power pulley on the tractor. Several neighbors arrived to help set up. With everything in readiness, Ward started the tractor and the big circular saw began to spin.

Father took his place at the left of the saw to determine the length of the blocks and throw them out of the way. Ward worked the saw table which slid the log against the whirring teeth. These two had the riskiest tasks. Carelessness could result in instant removal of a finger or more. Other men carried the logs from the pile to the saw. I moved the sawed blocks back out of the way towards the woodshed.

Completing the sawing took most of the day. At noon mother and grandma served a hearty meal to the men who had come to help. Father preceded the meal with a prayer of blessing on food and of petition for safety as they worked. Since this was fall, big wedges of mince and pumpkin pies added the crowning touch to the meal.

After dinner, Ward touched up the teeth of the big saw with a file to keep them sharp. Late that afternoon, when the tractor pulled out of the yard, saw rig in tow, my real work had only begun.

In the flurry of this activity, quite a number of pieces were cut too long for stove length. Also, some limbs were considered too small to run through the buzz saw. Dealing with these meant I had to cut them up with the buck saw. This instrument of torture consisted of a saw blade clamped into a rectangular wooden frame. The piece to be cut I placed on the saw buck which was constructed of two sets of wooden cross-pieces like big X's attached to each other at their centers. I pressed one foot on the limb to hold it in position. Grasping the saw with one hand at the top and the other on the handle at the base of the saw frame, I moved the blade back and forth. A more unnatural and wearying position could scarcely be devised. I thoroughly hated the buck saw.

Splitting and piling the wood for winter was an extended project which occupied much of my time between school and chores plus Saturdays as well. The kitchen range required wood more finely split than the heater which took fairly large chunks. My skill with the axe was such that only once did I ruin a boot and widen the slot between my big toe and its neighbor. The cut healed, but replacing the boot cost scarce dollars. When the woodshed was filled to the rafters, I stacked the balance in neat piles outside the woodshed door. In the fall we used first from these piles for the daily quota so the sheltered supply in the shed could serve when snow was deep.

Bringing in the wood was an at least twice daily task. I tried in vain to get father to build in a woodbox like Pratts had in their kitchen. This efficient device was a box which extended through both sides of the wall. The inside portion had a hinged lid which could be lifted to pick up a stick without going outside into the cold. The box was filled from the outside, avoiding the need to open a door. The arrangement was both practical and efficient.

We avoided burning unseasoned wood whenever possible. Not only did green wood make a poor fire if it burned at all, but it deposited creosote in the pipes and chimney. This tarry, black substance trickled in smelly rivulets down the stovepipe. Even more threatening, accumulations of creosote in the pipes and chimney could catch fire and burn fiercely enough to set the house ablaze.

One zero evening the Round Oak stove had been pushed to capacity to keep the house reasonably warm. Mother had pulled the shades and closed all doors to the living room in her attempt to conserve the warmth. Attuned to the sounds of the stove, father reacted to an unfamiliar roaring in the stove pipe.

Quickly closing all of the stove drafts, he dashed outside. The rest of us grabbed jackets and followed him. From the chimney belched flames and flying embers ten feet into the air. Fortunately the roof was buried deep in snow so the embers were quenched as they fell.

Grabbing the water pail, father called to me as he ran upstairs, "Pump two more pails of water and bring them up."

I found father standing guard upstairs with a dipper full of water in his hand. The stovepipe glowed cherry-red in the section where it passed through the floor and then entered the brick chimney. With a soaked cloth, father dampened the combustible wood nearest the pipe. Gradually the soot and creosote burned out, leaving only a few scorched boards as a warning.

"Thank the Lord!" father exclaimed, a sentiment that we all shared.

The Day Booth house had recently burned to the ground due to a chimney fire. Although our home was spared by father's prompt actions, for several weeks I had recurrences of the nightmares which had followed the schoolhouse fire.

On February 15, 1934, we awoke to find the thermometer at an unbelievable forty-four degrees below zero. For our valley, as well as the region, this set a new low record. At this very time father reached the conclusion that our wood supply would not last until spring. In looking for a handy source, father decided to cut two large elm trees which overshadowed the garden area and reduced the productivity of the plot. Elm was never a preferred stove wood due to the intertwining of its tough fibers, making it almost impossible to split. Oak, maple, ash, and beech were the trees of choice based on their burning qualities, ease of splitting, and availability in our area.

That Saturday morning, armed with cross-cut saw, axes, and wedges, we managed, with considerable effort, to fell the first tree. Making the saw blade run true without binding while in a horizontal plane added to the difficulty. Due to the very low temperature, the surrounding trees in the woods were resounding like rifle shots as their internal moisture froze and caused them to split.

Usually working the crosscut saw produced in the two participants a copious outpouring of perspiration. But not that morning! The remark was often made that wood was the wonder fuel, providing heat to those who cut it and again when it was burned. As I split, piled, and carried the wood, I believed that this could be multiplied again for each procedure.

With the tree felled, we chopped away the smaller limbs with an axe. Larger limbs we severed from the trunk with the cross-cut saw. Then the real work of sawing blocks from the main trunk began in earnest. Using a cross-cut saw required teamwork of a high nature. Each of the two operators grasped the wooden handle at their end of the six to eight foot blade. With a smooth reciprocating motion, one would draw the blade in his direction, while the other person deftly guided the other end to keep it from whipping. Then the roles reversed. Establishing and maintaining a steady pace for this action called for each to sense and adjust to the speed and length of the stroke. A skilled, matched team performed in a symphony of motion beautiful to behold. The blade would sink quickly into the deepening groove with the fall of sawdust an almost continuous alternating cascade from the singing teeth.

The pace did not go smoothly that morning. The old elm's rough fibers tended to make the blade draw hard and pinch. Father's longer arms and greater strength were no match for mine in spite of my best efforts.

"Arnold, do you need to ride the saw?" father complained. "Draw the blade back straight. You're curving it so it binds." "Why can't you keep up an even pace?" "Draw it out the full stroke." The cold and the urgency of the task kept us sawing although father's sharp criticism made the atmosphere strained.

Upon starting to split the blocks, we made a remarkable discovery. Due to the freezing action of the extremely low temperatures in this green wood, a deft axe blow split slabs readily without the need to resort to using wedges and the sledge. Lest the elm revert to its resistant ways with the return of milder weather, we finished the job that afternoon. In spite of the toughness of my palms from regular manual labor, I had king-size blisters by nightfall. The green wood didn't burn well and had to be combined with drier slabs to make a fire. When the last chunks disappeared into the stove, I had no regrets.

Production of light at the parsonage was not without a fair amount of effort. For me, it was an oft-recurring, little-loved routine. The kerosene lamp or lantern's yellow flame never produced enough lumens to easily read and do close work. Wicks developed an uneven spot which caused the flame to lick up the side of the glass chimney, depositing a layer of soot. Too high a flame had the same result. Filling the fuel tank required care, lest the flammable liquid be spilled, creating a fire hazard.

Every farm boy knew the potential of the smelly liquid from experience with using a small amount to start a fire in the stove. One morning I was asked to kindle the fire in the kitchen range. Invariably the kitchen fire went out over night. After placing newspaper and finely split kindling on the ashes, I decided to assure a fast start.

I poured a little kerosene over the prepared kindling. The match flamed as I struck it on the box and touched the paper. A sudden flash made the stove griddles dance. Ashes spewed out into the kitchen. The flash and minor explosion brought mother and grandmother on the run.

"Arnold. Are you all right?" mother wanted to know.

A bit calmer, grandmother assessed my damages. "Your eyebrows are singed and your arm looks like a singed chicken," she pronounced grimly.

"Don't tell father," I pleaded. "I promise to never use kerosene again to start the fire."

"We'll see," was their non-committal answer. But the subject was not broached later when father entered the kitchen.

Father made a marvelous acquisition which cast light on the dimly-lit evening scenes. To a boy who loved to read, the Aladdin lamp had a most appropriate name. Although it too burned kerosene, instead of a wick, it had one large, fragile mantle which glowed with a pure white light. A large chimney surmounted with a reflective glass shade concentrated the light. This was a contrast to the oil lamps whose yellow beams seemed to be absorbed by the dark which lurked in all corners of the room.

The light from this wonderful lamp changed our lives in other ways. Not only was study made easier for me, but during the long winter evenings mother began to read to the family from a variety of books, such as Burnett's *The Secret Garden* and *The Swiss Family Robinson.*

When supper was finished, Father brought up a pan of apples from the cellar - Baldwins, Nonesuch, Northern Spies, and Rome Beauties. While mother's reading made these exciting tales come to life, the rest of us peeled, cored, and sliced the crisp fruit to munch on as we paid close attention.

As mother ended a chapter, father noted our nods and tendency to drift towards unconsciousness. Firmly he pronounced, "It's bed time."

"Please. Just one more chapter," Irving and I begged.

"Let's save it for tomorrow night," father countered. And we knew it was a lost cause.

This precursor of radio and television did much to increase family unity and broaden our horizons.

As a compensation for the limited use of my feet, I became an omnivorous reader of any available book. All of the books in the limited school library I perused at least once, some of them many times. I still have one certificate which attests to my having read 41 library books in the 1931-32 school term.

Of all of the books in the school library, my favorite was "Arlo" by Bertha and Ernest Cobb, the tale of a little boy in the Alps who was kidnapped by Gypsies. He saved the kingdom for the Prince who turned out to be his father. The images it created of toasting cheese over a little fire high on an alp became etched in my mind. When District No. 6A merged in a consolidation, I contacted May Sprowl, the last teacher before that school was closed. She passed on to me the worn little blue volume which had provided me so much enjoyment.

One farm in the valley stood out from others. Gene Wing installed a Delco system consisting of a generator powered by a gasoline engine. The generator charged a bank of batteries and energized the first electric lights in the area. Two drawbacks were its cost and the limited amount of power it produced. The batteries quickly lost their charge when the noisy generator shut down and soon the lights dimmed. After our visits to their home, I dreamed of the day when I could just flip a switch and light would come forth without effort. But that was not to be our experience until we left the valley and moved to Gowanda in the fall of 1936.

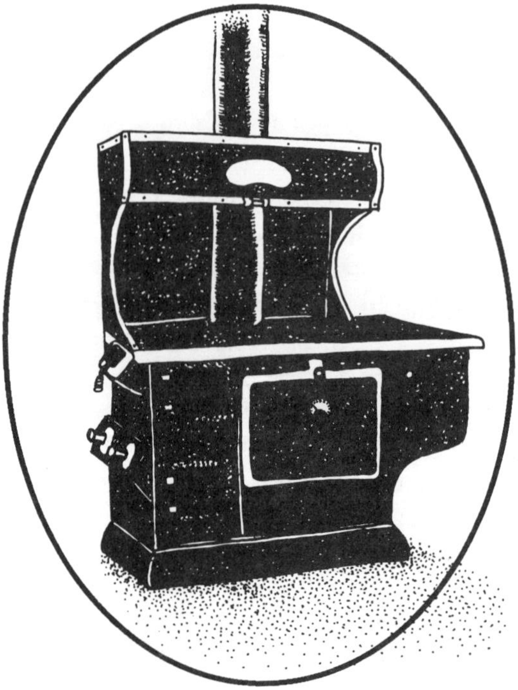

Robbery in the Potato Patch

"What came in the mail today?" father inquired as he returned from East Otto.

"Just the paper and two more seed catalogs," mother responded. "When you make out seed orders, grandma and I want to include some flower seeds," she reminded him. "Burpee has a new hybrid dahlia with striking colors."

The Great Depression did not mean undernourishment or lack of food for our family. While we were short of money, clothing, and physical possessions, adequate food was not among our deprivations. Living in the country and producing much of the essentials really made the difference. Frugality was a way of life which extended to the utilization of leftovers. Mother had mastered the art of making things stretch.

We always had an extensive garden. In midwinter the colorful catalogues from the seed companies arrived in our mailbox bearing names such as Burpee, Field, Crossman, and others. Father carefully compared the prices and characteristics of the seeds offered by competing companies before placing his orders.

This time of year also brought colorful offers from seed companies showing how prizes and/or money could be earned peddling seeds from door to door. These were aimed towards school children and showed happy boys and girls riding on shiny bikes they had earned through selling that company's seeds.

"Father, I want to sell seeds this year." I spoke ever so enthusiastically. "See the new bike I can earn. May I, please?" Several times I received parental permission to try my luck at salesmanship. Fired with hope and enthusiasm when the bundle of seed packets arrived for me in the mail, I trudged through the snow or rain of early spring to offer my wares to our neighbors. A few were kind enough to buy, but many just did not have the money with which to purchase the seeds that sold for five or ten cents per envelope. The limited number of households and the distance between houses in our rural area severely limited my success. If the company had not offered a generous return policy for unsold merchandise, the enterprise would have resulted in a loss. The dream of earning a new bike in this manner quickly faded.

Our own dairy products were there for the using: milk, cream, cottage cheese, and butter - except when we were short for customer orders. Although we produced eggs to sell, those not of marketable quality kept us supplied for home use. In addition to cracked eggs, other defects were sorted out through a process known as candling.

Father designed a home-made device for candling by cutting an egg-shaped hole in a piece of cardboard. Behind this hole he positioned a candle or oil lamp. As we held each egg up to this hole, the light shining through the translucent eggshell revealed imperfections such as blood spots. Eggs that failed this scrutiny were rejected and labeled as unmarketable. Next, we weighed each egg on an egg scale, as size of an egg is determined by weight, rather than physical dimensions. The peewees and the occasional super double-yolked specimens also went for family use. These provided an excellent source of protein.

The high cost of commercial fertilizers forced us to rely on the home-grown variety - manure - which we dubbed B-Y Brand for barn yard. On the first really warm day in mid-April, when the probability of frost had declined, mother announced firmly, "Father, it's time to plow the garden."

In addition to getting an early start on the growing season, mother had another motivation. Similar to many of the farmhouses, the cracks between the foundation stones permitted the winter winds to blow up under the floor. Father followed tradition in banking manure all around the outside perimeter of the walls to reduce drafts. In addition to reducing the drafts, the decomposition process itself produced some heat. Mother usually prevailed in delaying "banking up" in the fall until the weather was cold enough to minimize the odor. But, with the coming of warm spring days, the aroma increased. This triggered mother's exhortations to remove the banking and spread it on the garden. We augmented the manure from around the house with a fresh increment from the pile by the stable. Since we did not own horses, father was forced to await a time when one of the neighbors could spare a horse or team to plow the garden.

We grew the usual vegetables: peas, beans, beets, carrots, cabbage, tomatoes, corn, potatoes, cucumbers, pumpkins, and squash. Our attempts to grow melons and similar plants failed because frost always nipped them before they could mature. Planting the garden was interesting work.

"Arnold, don't plant the carrots too thick," father admonished.

My propensity to scatter the seeds thickly made the job finish sooner. Although temporarily concealed under the loose soil, my transgressions on this point came quickly to light as soon as the young plants pushed up through the ground.

"Look at those beets," father sputtered. "They're so close together we'll have to thin them. The seed could have made two rows."

When the plants emerged enough to be readily visible, my real work began - weeding and cultivating. For some perverse reason, the plot behind the house where we had our garden was prime quack grass territory. Give me ragweed, dock, or even thistles any day in preference to quack grass. It spreads underground by means of wiry roots, emerging like a green plague. Like the mythical Hydra, chopping off the top seemed to make it double its response. Pulling it seldom removed the deep, entwined roots. Every little broken piece remaining in the ground became a new plant. In our attempts to kill it, we sometimes spread in the road the basketfuls we had pulled.

Newly-sprouted vegetable plants had to be weeded by hand, This required great care lest removal of the weeds disturb the tender plants. Later, the hoe came into its own. This activity called for skill and precision. Just one careless chop of the hoe would wipe out the potential of a tomato plant.

Potatoes were an important crop. Grandma had emigrated from Ireland where these tubers formed an important staple in the Irish diet. Thriving potato vines attracted destructive beetles known as potato bugs. These little hard-shelled creatures proliferated rapidly if unchecked. Lacking modern pesticides, I was appointed protector of the spud crop. Armed with an old bucket and a wooden paddle, I walked slowly up and down the rows, knocking the bugs into the bucket. I also turned back the leaves, looking for the deposits of their bright orange eggs which, if allowed to hatch, soon re-infested the vines. Carefully I spared the colorful ladybugs which were beneficial in the control of aphids. After "beating the patch," I placed a wad of kerosene-soaked paper in the collection bucket and touched a match to it. Once more the potato crop was temporarily safe.

With successive plantings of peas, beans, and corn, the garden performed better than the produce counter at the grocery store, for there was immediate availability and unquestionable freshness. Arrival of unexpected company usually resulted in my receiving a "grocery list" to pick from the garden.

Except for lettuce and radishes, peas were the earliest vegetable. Grandmother strongly believed that new peas deserved to be served with new potatoes. She invaded the potato patch and dug into some hills to extract the growing tubers which had reached a diameter of one or two inches.

"Why don't you let them grow up?" father implored. "If allowed to mature, they would make a lot more eating."

"New peas should have some new potatoes to go with them," she insisted.

Father's arguments never deterred grandma from filching a few of the little red "marbles" as father referred to them. Scrubbed and boiled whole with the peas, they were then, and have always remained for me one of nature's gourmet delights. A big bowl of peas and new potatoes accompanied by freshly-baked bread constituted a complete and satisfying meal.

Mother baked almost all of our bread - large, golden-crusted loaves with real substance, nothing like the puffy store-bought product. Her bread tasted its very best while warm, the aroma of baking filling every corner of the parsonage. Thick slices, in my case spread with soft maple sugar in preference to butter, made a fitting example of its function as the "staff of life." Two batches weekly were required to feed our family, so it seldom grew stale or moldy even though it contained no preservatives.

Sometimes mother varied the recipe a bit. She fashioned part of the dough into large, fluffy rolls or into cinnamon buns studded with plump raisins. The latter were a real treat which made breakfast an anticipated meal.

Cakes, pies, and cookies also emerged from the old oven. Mother had a special knack for making pies: traditional apple, savory pumpkin, colorful cherry, scrumptious blackberry, and hearty mince from our own mincemeat. I still prefer pie to cake, even on my birthday!

One favorite kind of cookie she made by using the dough for sugar cookies. Half of the dough mother cut into round, scalloped shapes. The top halves matched but had a one-inch hole in the center. Mother ladled a sweet raisin filling onto the lower half and then covered it with the cutout part. She pressed the two parts together around the edge before baking. This sweet, moist treat the baking companies are still trying to match, but without success.

I liked the taste of the unbaked dough so well that mother had to curb my snitching the trimmings from the cutting board. With plenty of lard from our own hogs, mother often made batches of golden-brown fried cakes. I still have the old black iron doughnut kettle in which she heated the fat on top of the wood range.

As any good cook knows, the temperature of the oven is critical to the quality of the product. Control of the heat was not achieved by setting a thermostat, as the old range had no such device. Instead, judicious selection and knowledgeable application of sticks of wood to the fire produced the temperature variations. Knowing the characteristics of the various kinds of wood and the vagaries of the particular stove were essential skills required of every competent farm housewife.

Mr. Russell drove his panel truck from door to door through the countryside with basic groceries arranged on shelves along the sides. It constituted a convenience store on wheels. Hayden Silvernail, one of father's parishioners, took a job peddling bread from door to door from a small enclosed truck. These were just two examples of how men tried to develop a business when jobs were scarce.

Typical of the reaction of children was my lack of appreciation of present benefits. I demonstrated this bias by my craving bakery loaves instead of home-made bread. When Hayden Silvernail stopped at our house on his rounds, I begged, "Mother, please buy a loaf of bakery bread."

Silvernail peddled one kind of bread mother didn't make - salt rising. This moist, dense loaf exuded a unique, tangy odor. Toasted, it made excellent cheddar cheese sandwiches. Since father was partial to salt rising, mother bought a loaf for special occasions. The charge per loaf delivered to the house ran between eight and ten cents.

When he went to Springville, father sometimes brought home a big flour-sack full of stale bread and other baked goods which were sold for animal feed. We always salvaged some items for our own use before feeding the rest of it to the chickens and pigs. In this way, I experienced delicacies we would not have otherwise tasted. Sometimes we found cream puffs, strudels, and crullers.

During his years of study at Cleveland Bible Institute (now Malone College,) father had worked part-time for a cheese vendor at the Cleveland public market. From this exposure to a great variety of domestic and foreign cheeses, he had developed a discriminating taste for this dairy food. Periodically he took me in the old Chevy to the one remaining cheese factory in our area operating at the intersection of Maynard and Bowen Hollow Roads.

"Good morning, John," father greeted Mr. Lankow, who was both the cheese-master and the owner. "I'd like to buy a wedge of cheese. May we check some samples?"

"Come this way." We followed Mr. Lankow to the cool gloom of the curing room. Surrounded by round hoops of his aging product, with his special knife he cut thin slices from one cheese and then another. As he lifted the hoops of cheddar out of their special round basswood boxes, he laid back the cheesecloth coverings to reveal the texture. When he severed two samples of each, I was delighted to be included in the sampling process.

After tasting several samples, father spoke decisively: "Please cut about five pounds from this one. It has character."

Deftly the cheesemaster cut the requested amount, coming within an ounce or so. Wrapping it in heavy waxed paper, John Lankow remarked appreciatively, "Reverend, you chose a good one. It has outstanding flavor. I share your taste."

Canning involved much work in the gathering and preparation of the vegetables and fruits as well as in the actual processing. Lack of refrigeration often meant taking care of the perishables immediately lest they spoil. When the processing lasted into the late evening hours, father took my place and sent me off to bed. My help was often conscripted not only for gathering the produce, but for cutting up string beans, shelling peas, and cutting corn from the cobs. Pumping the quantities of water needed for the canning boiler was also my responsibility.

I much preferred peeling peaches, removing the pits, and packing the halves in jars, to pitting cherries or shelling peas. I opted for activities which permitted me to perform them sitting on the porch or out under the maple tree. Mother had the hot, steamy part which required working in the kitchen over the hot wood stove even on scorching summer or fall days.

From mother I acquired my dislike for several types of meat, especially chicken, which she never ate. She found it impossible to disassociate a pork chop or slice of roast beef from the animal that supplied it. Although we had ample meat, our consumption of protein and fat in this form was significantly less than that of our neighbors. In my eating preferences, as well as in other more significant ways, my wife's efforts to change me have been signally successful. In fact, I now enjoy many of the foods against which I held strong prejudices. One noteworthy exception still remains: cottage cheese.

In spite of having the ingredients readily available, ice cream was a rare treat. Without an ice cream freezer, we waited for the temperature outside to fall to zero or below.

"It feels like tonight is going to be super cold," father shivered as he came in from checking on a sick cow.

"Mother, please can we make ice cream tonight," I asked hopefully.

"Please, pretty please," Irving chimed in.

"If you'll help with stirring it," mother conceded.

After mother had prepared the custard, I carried it out to the front porch and covered it with a big kettle to keep out the cats, dogs, or other animals. Hurrying back into the house, we waited for a few minutes before Irving went out to stir it first. We traded off this cold task, stirring more frequently as it started to stiffen.

"I think its ready," I called. Mother sent grandmother to check it. With her confirmation, I carried the kettle inside. Dipping this "all natural" treat out into big cereal bowls, we drenched the icy mounds with maple syrup.

Jello was cheap and easy to make, so mother served this dessert frequently with canned fruit embedded in it. The Young Peoples Society of the church discovered a money-making source - selling jello and pudding mixes from the Anna Elizabeth Wade Company. The secret of this successful venture was the high quality and low price of the products. The price was half that of the leading brands. In addition, the list of flavors available rivaled Baskin and Robbins ice cream. No risk was entailed, as we took orders for later delivery. Favorites were orange-pineapple, blueberry, and banana-orange. The products sold themselves by word of mouth as the price stood at one dime per double box.

Don Sprowl and I did much of the order taking and delivery, carrying the products in wire baskets attached to the handle bars of our bikes. In winter, we hauled the cartons on our sleds, receiving a lot of healthy exercise while supporting a good cause.

As our family gathered around the table three times daily for meals, we were repeatedly reminded of tangible cause for giving thanks. Soup kitchens and food lines were not a part of our own depression experiences, although mother always fed any of the wandering homeless who occasionally found their way to our valley.

Maple Sugaring
Sweet Results From Hard Work

"Sap's running," father announced at breakfast. "Steinbars tapped last week - just in time."

Two days later on my way to school I observed clouds of white water vapor rising from three different sugar houses. The sound of maple sap dripping into buckets and the sight of man-made clouds of steam billowing up into the frosty air from rustic sugar houses were sure signals that spring had come to our valley. Some of my moments of keenest pleasure as a boy occurred as I shared in this harvesting of one of nature's finest gifts.

Several of the valley farmers had stands of hard maples in their woodlots which they tapped yearly to provide a seasonal source of much-needed income. Among that group were Steinbars, Woodards, Wings, and Pratts. Half way to East Otto, the Lincoln operation was by far the largest, as they used equipment, techniques, and marketing methods advanced for that era. While I went frequently up to Steinbars to see Preston, whose father's farm adjoined the parsonage acreage on the south, most of my contacts were with sugaring at Pratts, whose grandson, Don Sprowl, was my best friend.

The season usually began in early March and lasted into April, although a mild spell in February might signal time to start. When the warmth of the days caused thawing on the south side of the ridges and the nights dropped below freezing, Mother Nature conveyed the message to the trees that it was time to send the sap upward from the roots to the branches to prepare for the development of new leaves. A regular pattern of successive days of this thaw/freeze cycle prolonged the season. Too long a thaw with encouragement of bud development curtailed the suitable span for sap collection. The resultant product turned dark in color and tasted strong or "buddy." The uncertainty of the weather lent urgency to make syrup while the sap was running.

Central to the activity was the sugar house, usually a weather-beaten structure of unpainted boards built like a shed but with this tell-tale difference: the roof was in the form of a louvered cupola designed to keep out the rain and snow but permitting the water vapor to escape in clouds of steam. The location varied by farm. The ideal position for the sugar house was near enough the farmhouse for easy monitoring of the boiling process, yet reasonably handy to the trees from which the sap was extracted. Inside was the arch or fire box over which big pans were connected by pipes to one another. Outside, the large storage tanks were piped to the inner boiling pans.

Preparation began long before the sap started to flow. An adequate supply of wood was prepared by felling trees, cutting them to length to fit the huge firebox, and hauling them to the sugar house where they were stacked high by the door. Buckets which had been stored in the sugar house were washed to remove accumulated dirt. At the close of the prior season they had been put away without washing, as the sticky sap tended to make a protective coating which retarded rust. Metal spouts with wire hangers were assembled and bits of the proper diameter were sharpened for use with the hand auger.

Sometimes the farmers tried to anticipate the weather, relying on the Farmers' Almanac or their intuition. Extra help was often needed for the tapping process. The supply of buckets, spouts, and other paraphernalia was brought to the woodlot on a pair of bobs drawn by a team of horses. Depending on the tree diameter, one or more holes were drilled about waist-high in the trunk of each sugar maple with a hand auger. A spout with hook attached was driven into the hole and a bucket hung from the hook.

Often metal covers were attached to the tops of the buckets to keep out rainwater. If tapped too early or if the season lasted longer than usual, the holes closed over and re-tapping became necessary. In later years, it was discovered that insertion of a formaldehyde "pill" into the hole before driving in the spout delayed this re-growth process and avoided re-tapping. Turning the hand auger to bore the holes was hard work while standing on the slippery slopes.

Recognition of the sugar maple from other varieties of trees was essential to the tapper. Making an identification error was cause for good-natured ribbing of the culprit.

"Did you hear that Lloyd Sprowl tapped a walnut tree?" the story would circulate.

"Must be he wanted to have walnuts in his maple sugar," the hearer wisecracked.

When weather conditions cooperated and afforded the right mix, sap dripped freely out of the spouts into the buckets. Rate of flow varied based on weather, starting and stopping as the cycle of freezing and thawing took place. As soon as a spot check revealed that buckets were getting full, gathering began. The team of horses was harnessed to a specially-constructed sled on which the large galvanized collecting tanks were installed. In some instances the running gear was not pure sled, but a hybrid with wheels in front and runners behind. The degree to which snow covered the tracks through the woods affected the relative efficiency of runners versus wheels.

At Pratts, the woods covered the hill north of the sugar house. Passage of the crude sled through the sugar bush, as the woods was referred to, had, over the years, created vestiges of roads. Reducing the distance sap had to be carried from the trees to the collecting tank saved time and effort. Each person involved in this part of the work carried a large pail into which they emptied the buckets of sweet sap. Then they lugged full pails back to the sled and poured them into the tank. The trained team of horses moved the tank along with a minimum of direct control by the driver. Voice commands were sometimes direction enough.

I found that carrying heavy pails of sap up or down slushy, icy, or muddy sidehills utilized many of my muscles in ways to which they were unaccustomed. I wore knee-high rubber boots, the regulation footgear. When I slipped while carrying a full pail of sap, the icy fluid cascaded down the open tops of my boots. The result was startling thrills and chills.

On a warm day, with the chickadees calling and the smells of spring in the air, I enjoyed the gathering process. On days when sleet or fog enveloped the valley, or when a chill rain was driven by the wind, the physical discomforts soon turned the job into drudgery. Surprises occasionally spiced up the routine. In some buckets I discovered a mouse or other rodent that drowned while attempting to sample the sweet liquid.

When the gathering tanks were full, the rig was driven to the top of the knoll above the sugar house. To save the time and effort of driving down to the sugar house, the tanks were emptied into a pipeline carrying the sap down to the main storage tank. Gravity took care of that portion of the journey. When warm weather caused the sap to flow freely, keeping up with the collecting and having adequate storage space became problems. Then buckets overflowed and the valuable fluid seeped into the ground. This was the situation one March weekend as I accompanied father over to help Pratts with the gathering.

"Hi, Don. I can stay all day," I greeted my friend.

"We sure can use your help," he replied. "Let's go out to the sugar house.

Boiling had been going on through the night, so the inside of the sugar shanty was full of sweet humidity. The vapor rising from the boiling pans reduced visibility to about two feet as the roof louvers couldn't accommodate the volume of water vapor. Outside, the breeze grabbed portions of the spiraling plume, breaking it up into little clouds which quickly evaporated in the clear blue sky.

I followed Albert Pratt as he checked the float valve which controlled the level of the sap in the boiling pans, releasing just enough to keep them comfortably full. The series of connected pans directed the sap to the first pan where the contents were just as it came from the tree. As it flowed into sequential pans, the heat evaporated water and concentrated the bubbling liquid.

Grandpa Pratt tested the front pan for thickness. "How about a sample?" he suggested, scooping out a generous portion in an old tin dipper which he kept hanging on the wall. Don and I carried the steaming dipper outside to a snow bank into which we placed it to cool. Then we took turns savoring the amber syrup. Never did it taste better than under these circumstances in this setting.

Going back inside we were just in time to see Don's grandfather turning the spigot to draw off the syrup into a milk can. Expert knowledge involving temperature and consistency was required to know the precise moment when it was ready. From time to time the operator skimmed off impurities which came to the surface of the bubbling pans. On the average, it took forty gallons of sap to produce one gallon of syrup. Thirty-nine gallons of water had to be evaporated away to obtain the one gallon of product. Sugar content varied somewhat between individual trees.

With the pans refilled to proper capacity, Albert Pratt opened the big iron doors of the arch through which he fed fuel into the fire. Don and I carried lengths of dry wood for him to stoke the blaze. Maintaining the fire required skill to keep the pans boiling without becoming so hot that the syrup scorched and spoiled. The operator had to be constantly alert.

Don and I enjoyed basking in the warm, steamy atmosphere of the sugar house. We helped stoke the fire and assisted in other ways. With the sap running so heavily, filling all of the storage, boiling was to be continued into the night.

"Father, please let me stay to help Don at the sugar house tonight," I pleaded as he was getting ready to go home for chores.

"We'll see that Arnold gets home before too late," Grandpa Pratt added his support to the idea. To that, father agreed.

After helping Don with his chores, we ate supper around their big table before returning to the sugar shanty. Sharing in tending the boiling process was in some strange way satisfying to the senses. The ghost-like appearance of the scene as viewed through the vapor mist, the moist, sweet aroma caressing nostrils and taste buds, the glow of the crackling logs casting ruddy shadows on faces and momentarily reaching out into the dark corners created a feeling of camaraderie that was special.

Conversation flowed uninhibited between good friends. Don and I talked of kites, and fishing, and camping out. At this stage it was boy talk, for girls were not yet a topic of interest. Future occupation, travel, hopes and dreams we shared without reserve, without posturing. As we watched the glow of the embers, even the periodic silences strengthened our bond.

Far before drowsiness overtook me. Don's father emerged from the steamy background to announce, "Arnold. We promised your father to have you home no later than ten."

"Some time I'd like to stay 'till midnight," I wistfully responded.

At other times we ate lunch in the sugar house. Ordinary food tasted better in that setting. We anointed home-made bread still hot from the oven with warm syrup from the old dipper. The result was sticky but satisfying. Another fun thing was to place eggs in the sap until they were hard-boiled. Through osmotic diffusion, the flavor and sweetness of maple permeated the eggs. The result was a delectable variation impossible to describe to the uninitiated.

The syrup leaving the sugar house in milk cans was not ready for sale. In the Pratt kitchen, Don's mother and grandmother heated and purified the syrup, bringing the product to standard specifications for weight and density. Pure maple syrup weighs approximately eleven pounds per gallon compared to eight pounds for water.

They poured the boiling hot syrup into tinned gallon and half-gallon cans, screwing the metal caps on tightly to seal out air and keep the syrup from spoiling. On each can they glued a colorful orange label identifying the maker's name and address as required by law. Finally the finished product was ready to market. Pratts had established such a reputation for fancy quality that they always had standing orders for most of their production.

Syrup was only one of the end products from this marvelous tree. Further boiling down of the syrup made possible the creation of solid maple candy. It was poured into molds of various shapes, of which the maple leaf was the favorite. An intermediate stage between syrup and solid created what was known as soft sugar. About the consistency of stiff peanut butter, it was my favorite to spread on warm, fresh home-made bread or to sweeten the cracked wheat cereal for breakfast. Usually this was stored in emptied tin coffee cans. With a thin layer of syrup over the top to seal out the air, the soft sugar kept for long periods without molding.

One evening Pratts invited the parsonage family to supper after chores were done. After roast beef, gravy, mashed potatoes, peas, and bread, Don's mother and grandmother retired to the kitchen to prepare the special dessert. Soon they returned bearing large cereal bowls half-filled with hot syrup. This had been heated to a precise state as determined by testing it with a loop made from a broomstraw.

Spoon in hand, each person vigorously stirred the sticky contents of his bowl. After a few minutes, it turned a light brown and was transformed into a semi-solidified form, setting up much in the consistency of fudge. Cutting or breaking off pieces, we leisurely ate it. For rich dessert, this creation was in a league of its own. The uninitiated sometimes found it too sweet to eat in that quantity.

Nellie Pratt disliked people who put on airs and looked down on farmers. One such visiting minister had been invited to supper along with the pastor and his family. When the syrup for stirring into soft sugar was passed to him, he attempted to imitate the procedure being followed by the rest of the diners. After everyone else soon had completed the transformation, his dish remained as fluid as it started out. Nellie Pratt suggested that he stir it in the opposite direction. He did so. Still no change. After he had tried several other suggestions, Albert Pratt took pity on him, explaining the difference. The preacher had been given a dish of warm Karo syrup. Although it looked like the maple, no amount of stirring would convert it into soft maple sugar.

At church, when father announced a youth party for Saturday night at Pratts, I guessed correctly what refreshments would be served. "Wax on snow" was one further maple variant traditional to the Brooklyn valley. After games and other activities, we gathered in the kitchen where Lula Sprowl had heated the syrup to the critical point for wax.

Dishpans full of clean snow which Don had carefully gathered from snowbanks were set on crates around the room. Don's mother drizzled the heated syrup in golden cascades over the surface of the snow in the pans. As it struck the surface of the cold snow, it changed into the consistency of taffy.

Forks in hand, several boys and girls clustered around each

pan. Rolling the sticky "wax" onto the tines, they transferred the icy sweetness to their mouths where it literally melted. As competing forks cleared the pocked surface, Don's mother applied more until the prepared syrup was exhausted. During most sugaring seasons, nature obliged by leaving enough protected snowbanks to make possible this ancient rite of spring.

First-run syrup was the best quality - light amber and with a delicate flavor. As the season advanced, the syrup produced was progressively darker, until it reached the stage where it acquired a strong taste. Buds starting to show on the maples signaled the end of the season. To protect the reputation of their syrup, Pratts would not market for retail this darker syrup, but sold it in bulk to a processor. Years later, while working in Burlington, Vermont, I discovered that this low-grade New York State maple syrup was purchased by Penick & Ford, Ltd. This firm shipped the darker syrup in fifty-five gallon drums to Burlington where they mixed it with cane syrup to create "Vermont Maid" syrup.

Another regular quantity purchaser of maple syrup was the Carey Maple Syrup Company of St. Johnsbury, Vermont. In 1935 they bought about two thousand gallons from farmers in the East Otto area at an average price of one dollar per gallon. They had four grade standards: Fancy, First, Second, and Third. The top grade was "suitable for fine hotels and Pullmans." The lowest grade was used in the "manufacture of rum and tobacco."

Father was usually called upon to help with sugaring at the Pratt farm. Customary remuneration for his work was to "give the parson a run." That is, the output of one of the runs of sap was his pay for helping. This was made up into whatever combination my parents preferred. Although much of it was in the form of syrup, a fair quantity of soft sugar in coffee tins constituted the balance. This barter of work for product created a sweet deal for both parties.

As much as I appreciated participation in sugaring at Pratts, I still wanted to try making some on my own. One spring I was successful in working out the necessary arrangements. Although there were no sugar maples on parsonage land, just west of our property a row of large maples lined the road across from Charles Wing's house. I asked for and received permission from Gene Wing, whose sugaring operation was so far from this stand that he never bothered tapping them. Don got his grandfather to lend me two dozen buckets and spouts. Armed with father's bit and brace, I tapped my trees and hung the buckets. Under the favorable weather that spring, the sap flowed generously.

Depending on the amount of snow, I dragged my sled or coaster wagon up the road daily to collect the run in large pails. Mother had agreed to let me boil it down on the kitchen range at times when it didn't interfere with cooking and baking. This part of the process worked all right in reducing the sap to syrup. But the water vapor it produced in quantity loosened the wallpaper in the kitchen. This problem started to spread to the dining room.

"Arnold. This can't continue," mother pronounced with justifiable severity. "Unless you can find another place to do the boiling, you'll have to give up the project."

The sugaring operation was duly evicted and I finished up my syrup season boiling the sap down on a fire in the yard where I supported the kettle on some stones.

As I poured "my syrup" over cooked wheat cereal, somehow it seemed to me that the syrup I had so laboriously produced was the best I had ever tasted. Nevertheless, once was enough - I decided that even these satisfying results didn't warrant the effort. And, more important, I missed Don's comradeship in the warmth of the sugar house.

In later years when Don sold the family farm and moved to Virginia, the old door from the sugar house was too personal a record to leave behind. Jackknives had carved into its rough surface hieroglyphics which, if later generations could correctly decipher, would tell tales of happy spring activities in Brooklyn valley.

Flivver Frailties: Soapstones and Laprobes

Under the heading, INTERESTING NEWS FROM EAST OTTO AND VICINITY, appeared the following news item in the March 16, 1931 issue of "THE CATTARAUGUS TIMES."

> "Albert Pratt accompanied Rev. Elmer Cook and son who motored to Springville on business on Saturday."

That doesn't sound very interesting. But wait! That wasn't the entire story. I know, for I was there. I was that son. Let me fill you in on what really happened.

The DeLaval cream separator had malfunctioned, and father was sure he had found the problem. To correct it required a small part obtainable from the dealer in Springville, only ten miles away by road. In church on the prior Sunday, Albert Pratt had mentioned to father that he needed to get to Springville to purchase a Cyclone grass seeder for the meadow. Having no telephone, father drove over to the Pratt farm to see if the trips could be combined, saving cost and energy. Soon Albert Pratt was ready, and I was relegated to the back seat of the 1928 Chevrolet for what sounded like an uneventful jaunt to town.

The old four-cylinder engine propelled the vehicle along at an unexciting pace as the two friends talked about weather, crops, and prospects for attracting new families to the church. One subject they never discussed was politics, as Albert Pratt was one of the few Democrats in the valley while father preferred the Republican party. My mind was more on the possibility that Albert Pratt might give me a nickel to spend for an ice cream cone than it was on their conversation. The clatter of the engine and the rattle of the hood covers in response to the frequent bumps formed a background of sound, a function supplied by today's Walkman.

Turning east at the church, we drove past the parsonage, over Brooklyn bridge, and on past the Cannoiserauley Road. Father didn't consider taking this shortcut which saved over three miles, as the road looked in bad condition and the very steep grade at the bottom of the hill made a right-angle turn difficult to negotiate even under better conditions. For similar reasons he had not chosen to take the Zoar Valley route up over Hammond Hill, for the steep descent to the Cattaraugus Creek included the Devil's Elbow, an infamous curve that almost turned back on itself in mid-grade.

The road was paved as far as its intersection with the one coming from Ashford Hollow. At this junction, we turned in a north-westerly direction on the Springville Road (now Route 219), which was also paved as far the cheese factory. As it turned northeast towards the Breakers, that section was "unimproved." Decidedly a euphemistic understatement that day. The two days prior had been warm, producing a thawing condition. During the previous night, the temperature had dropped into the twenties, freezing the surface to a depth of two or three inches.

Shortly we reached a portion of the road where "the bottom had gone out." The Chevy stayed on top of the lightly-frozen surface long enough to be well into the troublesome section. The wheels suddenly crunched through the frozen crust but failed to reach through the underlying mud to a solid surface. Quickly the car ground to a halt, as forward momentum waned. Father shifted into low and applied the gas. The frame was suspended on the crust so the back wheels churned helplessly. He tried reverse, with the same result. The car was thoroughly mired.

With no AAA to call, salvation by works appeared to be the only possible alternative. Following an earnest consultation, Albert Pratt waded through the mud to the old rail fence which bordered the highway. Here was emergency help. Using one fence rail as a fulcrum, a second as a lever, Albert Pratt was able to raise one wheel enough so father could place a third rail in the rut under the wheel. After repeating this three more times, all wheels had solid footing and the frame cleared the road surface. Positioning each of us at opposite rear corners, father told us to push hard when he put the Chevy in gear and gunned it.

It worked. Simultaneously the rear wheels had traction and the car lurched forward about twenty feet before again breaking through and settling in up to the axles. The spinning rear wheels had accomplished more: Mr. Pratt and I were both clobbered with the mud they had thrown up. For once, my glasses were unbroken, although covered with mud and dirty water which ran down our faces. Our clothes were well-spattered with the sticky stuff.

The same laborious process was repeated several times during which we accumulated even more of the earth's surface which attached itself to our clothing and persons. Over an hour later we had made it through the quagmire and reached solid footing. We continued down the sharp grade of the Breakers, over the steel bridge spanning the Cattaraugus Creek, and ground up the other side into Springville. Before reaching town, we stopped at a farmer's watering trough by the road, broke the ice, and cleaned up as best we could. Both men carried out their business transactions, as a journey at such expense was not to be wasted.

The return trip benefitted from the prior experience. Father gunned the Chevy through the troublesome area at a fairly fast pace, keeping one set of wheels in the center of the road and the other pair far to the side, thus avoiding the deep ruts. The car careened from side to side, throwing out mud behind like a dirty geyser, but made it through to the homeward side. With heartfelt thanks, father exclaimed, "Praise the Lord." Albert Pratt affirmed this sentiment with a hearty,

"Amen."

When we reached home, mother wanted to know why we had taken so long and why my good shoes were a mess. I don't know what Mrs. Pratt said to her husband. However, the account of our trip which she relayed to the local newspaper correspondent produced the innocuous one-line item quoted at the beginning of this truthful recitation of what had really happened. Indeed there are two ways of telling a story!

Not only did the roads of that era make travel by auto an undertaking fraught with uncertainty and discomfort, but the mechanical crudeness of the vehicles themselves left much to be desired. Two-wheel mechanical brakes afforded only limited ability to slow the car quickly. Operated by vacuum from the engine, the windshield wiper (normally only one) ceased its alternating movement when the motor was called upon to exert itself, such as in climbing a hill or passing another vehicle. To get a fleeting glimpse of what lay ahead meant letting off on the gas long enough for the wiper to make a swipe or two to clear the vision.

Defrosters for removing condensation or frost from the inside of the windshield didn't exist. Wiping or scraping by hand to maintain a peephole through which to see the highway constituted an ongoing battle with the elements. I recall father's driving home from afternoon service at Ashford Hollow on a zero Sunday afternoon with his head out the side window trying to keep in the road. In later years small electric fans with rubber blades were introduced to move the air, but they did nothing to provide heat.

Every two or three months we had to make the two-hundred mile trip to Utica to the foot specialist. Given the roads and cars of the time, the journey in each direction required a full day of travel. The winter trips were especially arduous, as our car did not have a heater. Father obtained a kit consisting of sheet metal parts which were designed to enclose the manifold portion of the engine. Father cut a hole in the firewall and connected it to the shrouding with a tube. The objective of this Rube Goldberg device was to direct some of the engine heat back into the passenger compartment. Without a fan, the warmth it delivered was minuscule. As a heater, it was a failure. In addition, the engine fumes made our eyes and noses weep.

Standard equipment for serious winter travel included the soapstone and the lap-robe. The former was a flat rectangular rock an inch or two thick. The special characteristic of this type of rock was its ability to retain heat. Some of these soapstones were equipped with wire handles for easier carrying. Well in advance of departure, we placed the soapstone on top of the stove or in the oven to heat. At the last minute, we wrapped it in newspaper and placed it on the floor of the vehicle so passengers could rest their feet on top of it. Due to the need for free movement in shifting gears and braking, the driver had little opportunity to benefit from such an arrangement. Early in a trip, the soapstone was too hot to rest one's feet on it. Eventually all heat was lost and it became just a cold stone.

We tucked heavy blankets made of rough wool in around our feet and pulled them up over our laps - hence the name, lap-robe. They also helped to capture some of the warmth emanating from the soapstones. For longer trips in extreme weather, we placed a lighted kerosene lantern under the lap-robe. In addition to the obvious hazards of getting burned or scorching clothing or robe, the fumes from the lantern irritated eyes and nose and left one's clothing inoculated with the pungent odor of kerosene. Although the lantern also presented a theoretical threat of asphyxiation, the body of our vehicle always permitted a generous amount of outside air to enter. Heavy winter clothing including boots, cap, scarf, and mittens were standard for winter travel. Women and girls often inserted their hands into fur muffs to keep them warm.

In those days, the 40,000 mile tire was not even a part of science fiction. Not only changing a tire but also the ability to repair one on the road were requisite driver skills. The clincher tires used on some vehicles required hard labor with primitive tools. Once the tire was repaired, inflating the tube with the puny gasps from a hand pump called for large inputs of time and effort. Tires were so poor that for longer trips father carried along extra ones tied to the normal spare.

By current standards, the trouble-free life of an engine was expensively short. Major repairs such as grinding the valves, putting new rings on the pistons, and replacing the rod and main bearings were normal occurrences. Our Chevy was subject to these ailments and several times had its internal organs spread on the barn floor for healing or transplant. Father was always alert to any warning knock, rattle, clatter, or burst of smoke from the exhaust which exceeded the norms. Such symptoms usually preceded a spell of walking for a week or so while repairs were attempted. On our small income, such bouts with mechanical failure also produced financial crises.

The roof of our Chevy was typical of cartops of those days in that it was not made of metal. Rather, it was composed of heavy fabric stretched over wooden ribs attached to the body. Regular attention was required to keep it waterproof, as weathering caused the roof to crack or become porous. Father applied a black liquid top dressing at frequent intervals as a prudent exercise of preventive maintenance.

Father often needed to carry things which wouldn't fit inside of the car. He draped bags of feed over the fenders and laid them on the running board. The Chevy had no trunk, as the spare tire occupied that position at the rear of the car. Father wedged two oak boards between the rear bumpers and the frame. On these projections, he constructed a wooden platform for carrying luggage or feed bags. For trips to Utica, he fastened grandma's old steamer trunk to the rack, covering it with a canvas tarp. Although it didn't look stylish, this improvisation met an urgent need.

Auto expenses constituted the largest demand on our limited cash, for the Chevy served as an integral part of the church ministry. Driving miles over country roads, by times dusty, snowy, or muddy, was one way in which father made it possible for people to attend Sunday School and church. Many of them were too poor to have their own transportation. Never did father consider bringing people to church as an imposition. Instead, he viewed this as part of his outreach to the valley which he served as conference missionary.

As a boy, I didn't view things from his perspective. How I longed for a better car such as those I observed others driving. Don's father, Lloyd, worked at the Willis Garage in Cattaraugus, the local Ford agency. He traded regularly for a new model. Chris Steinbar, whose land adjoined ours, also traded frequently. Rev. Wesley Parmerter, the District Elder who came to check on the circuit, drove one of the new makes - a Plymouth which was touted as having "floating power." And the man who motored out from Buffalo on Saturdays to purchase butter sported a substantial Buick.

I pored over the colorful advertisements for the new models

which sounded marvelous. Of all of these mechanical wonders, I was most enthralled with the sleek lines and impressive grille of the 1935 Reo Flying Cloud. To me, it was a thing of consummate beauty. The name REO was derived from the initials of its inventor, R. E. Olds, whose name has endured in GM's Oldsmobile. History has disproved his claim that the Flying Cloud represented the ultimate in auto technology and design to which no improvements could be made. However, it still was a great automobile.

These boyhood dreams still evoke nostalgic memories whenever I view one of these great cars of the Thirties displayed in an auto museum. I now realize that the simple, uncomplicated, tough old Chevy was better suited than most of the others for father's purposes in carrying out his ministry to the valley.

Wet Canvas, Straw Ticks, and the Sawdust Trail

One Sunday in early June father's announcements at the little white Brooklyn church extended longer than usual.

"Be sure to set aside July 9 through 18 for our annual district camp meeting," father emphasized. Then he went on with details of place, times of services, and costs. He had the ushers pass out folders with pictures of the guest speakers and singers.

Camp meeting was an institution in which father believed fervently. His conviction of its importance never wavered in the half-century he spent in the ministry. The fact that it was special to him affected the way I related to camp meeting. The views presented here reflect my boyish perspective on this period of special spiritual emphasis conducted in an outdoor setting.

Although camp meeting came as close to a family vacation as any experience we had, marked differences differentiated it from the typical vacation. Looking back, I now realize that vacation was a concept father never embraced in practice. In our district of the Free Methodist Church, the normal time for scheduling this event was early July. Effort was made to set camp meeting for the interval between haying and harvest to encourage farm families to attend.

Father's promotion of this ten-day meeting went far beyond just announcing it to his congregation. He personally encouraged individuals and families to attend. If some of the young people of the community could not afford to go, father made their attendance possible by including them in our family group.

Instead of having a fixed place for holding the camp, in those days the location varied from year to year. A suitable wooded area was identified and permission for its use was obtained from the owner. Forestville, South Dayton, Lawtons, Randolph, Machias, and Cattaraugus were all chosen at one time or another. Eventually, in later years, Cattaraugus was selected for the permanent site. Father was always among those who volunteered to prepare the grounds. He volunteered my help too.

Upon arrival at the new camp site early on the first work day, I jumped out of the Chevy and began my own tour of the premises. I had ideas of what constituted a preferred site for our family tent. Having located my first choice, I hurried back to the car to get our ax and bucksaw to start clearing the spot.

"Arnold. We need your help over here," father called from where men were at work removing the brush and small trees to create an open area large enough to erect the tabernacle.

"Can't I get a place ready for our tent first?" I pleaded. "I've found the perfect site and someone else will take it if I don't get it staked out first."

"First things first," father reminded me with one of his sayings to which I had been exposed many times. "There will be plenty of chance after the tabernacle is up." I knew that further argument was useless and went to work clearing brush from the tabernacle site.

The actual erection of the big tent required synchronizing the efforts of all available hands. I was delegated the job of holding one of the ropes as the two center poles were raised aloft and secured with guy ropes.

Will Manning, who had taken charge of erecting the big tent, shouted, "Everyone in position! Up it goes."

The big expanse of canvas rose up the poles as men tugged on the ropes attached to pulleys. Once the center of the tent was raised to its proper position, those of us holding ropes around the perimeter pulled the canvas out to its extremity. Others wielding heavy mauls pounded big stakes into the ground and tied each rope securely. The tabernacle was up for one more season.

Just as I was poised to dash off to our intended site, father directed me to help spread the load of sawdust which had just arrived. Donated by a local sawmill, a layer of sawdust was spread on the ground under the tabernacle. Its function was to keep the area clean and reduce the dust bound to be raised over the ten day period by many trampling feet. I rather enjoyed working at this task with other children. The men were too busy to chide us for throwing sawdust and putting handfuls inside someone's shirt.

Before the sawdust was all distributed, a local farmer drove his team and wagon up to the front of the tabernacle.

"Help unload the straw," was my next directive.

The loose straw was brought in to be available for anyone needing to fill straw ticks for beds. Some people also used it to cover the floor of their tent. Before one job was completed, someone always appeared to conscript my help at another urgent project. Folding benches which had been stored needed to be dusted off and placed in orderly rows throughout the tabernacle. When father finally released me, I discovered that someone else had already set their tent on the site I had wanted.

In one respect I was fortunate. I kept busy enough with other jobs to avoid being asked to help dig the trenches for the latrines. Usually the intertwining of tree roots and rocks made this excavation project difficult. Multi-hole seats were constructed over the pits. Two specially-modified tents were erected to provide a degree of privacy. Ignoring the direction of prevailing winds sometimes resulted in errors of placement of these "necessary booths." Before the ten days had passed, all attending became increasingly aware of such errors of judgment.

While all of this was happening at the site of the coming camp, preparation at home proceeded simultaneously. Mother and grandmother baked, cooked and gathered produce from the garden.

They assembled canned fruits and vegetables from the basement, as well as bedding, towels, and all of the items necessary for basic living. On the day of our departure, organized confusion reigned as we loaded the Chevy and trailer with tent, bedsprings, crates of food, an old oil stove, and what seemed like an endless array of necessities. Scarcely was there room remaining for the people to sit. We looked like a bunch of Gypsies to anyone who glimpsed our overloaded vehicles.

This year camp meeting was located at South Dayton. We left the parsonage at Brooklyn with the rumblings of distant thunder grumbling over the hills.

"I think we're going to be caught in a thunderstorm," mother worried out loud.

"Eva, don't fret. I think it will pass south of us. We won't get more than a sprinkle," father reassured her.

Grandma didn't agree with father. "Elmer, everything is going to get soaked."

But father was in the driver's seat. Rumblings in the sky and in the back seat escalated as we passed through Otto.

Coaxing all of the speed the overloaded Chevy could muster, father was negotiating the steep hill into Cattaraugus just as the thunderstorm burst upon our equipage. The brightness of the lightning flashes was matched with almost immediate detonations of thunder. Fierce gusts swirled the drenching rain against the car. Water spurted into the car around the cracks of the doors and windows. The wind swayed the car and pelted the vehicle with twigs and small branches.

Satisfied that our unwieldy load had suffered as much water penetration as possible, the storm moved on in the direction of Little Valley. Water stood six inches deep on the level as we continued our journey. Even father was remarkably quiet. Mother passed up the opportunity to say, "I told you so!" The storm had completely missed the grove at South Dayton. Nevertheless, setting up a sodden tent and salvaging food and other perishable items made this a rough start for an extended encampment.

We used some old woven-wire springs set up on wooden blocks as our camp beds. In lieu of mattresses, I was handed the striped ticks, damp from the storm, to fill with straw at the tabernacle. I had learned from experience this was not a task at which to shirk, for plumper was better. I tried to avoid getting sticks or other hard objects mixed in with the straw. Fluffed up for the first night, the straw mattresses weren't too bad. But after the passage of a few days, lumpy spots and thin areas developed to the discomfort of the sleeper. Too, it seemed that on each succeeding night the sag in the springs became more pronounced as the bed took on the configuration of a hammock.

Our family food preparation and eating took place under an open canopy or fly at one end of the tent. Due to father's generosity, mother usually had ten or more for whom to prepare meals. The old oil stove had to serve as water heater for all purposes as well as for cooking. Preparing meals taxed even mother's resourcefulness. In fair weather, feeding the group was not easy, while in rainy spells the discomfort level skyrocketed. Sitting on benches around the rough wooden table, the diners were exposed to wind-driven rain. Towards the end of the period, baked items and other supplies ran low and the lack of variety in meals became noticeable. Although the fare was plain, no one went hungry.

At camp, rain was always the nemesis. In wet weather, any object or person just touching the wet canvas provided a route for the water to come inside the tent. So closely arranged were the beds that keeping the bedding from touching the tent sides was impossible. One showery afternoon I perched on my bed and watched a muddy stream course down through the center of the tent, carrying with it the straw floor I had so carefully laid.

Rain made the crude roadways through the woods a muddy morass in which cars became mired. After a series of rainy days at the end of a camp session, packing up the soggy stuff to take home tested all of the grace derived from attending ten days of camp services.

Close proximity to trees always held the potential for limbs to fall on the tents. Lightning posed a more deadly threat. During a heavy thunderstorm the year that camp was held at Lime Lake, one of the ministers, Rev. C. L. Fairbanks, was struck by lightning while in his tent. Although not fatal, it came as a real shock.

The time devoted to providing for the physical necessities was dwarfed by the allotted hours for meetings. Ringing of a bell by hand announced each service. The first bell in the morning called the faithful to prayer at six. Various types of meetings were held throughout the day, culminating in the evening service. As active as father and mother were with work and participating in the meetings, I don't know how they kept such close account of my attendance. But they did! Not for a moment would I minimize the primary importance of camp meeting as a time for crisis commitment and renewal in the lives of many individuals. However, the passage of time has brought about a better balance between evangelism, worship, study, meditation, and recreation than was true in the Thirties.

We still found time for activities with other children of our own age whom we saw infrequently except at camp. Ball games and other sports such as horseshoe pitching had a role. Early in the camp session, Stan Parmerter, the ace horseshoe-pitcher, caught one of the steel shoes in his forehead. He sported a bandage around his head for the remainder of camp.

We sought the coolness of Conewango Creek which flowed through the pasture near the camp. Unpleasant consequences struck while a group of us were wading in the stream, Ralph Crowell scrambled out on the bank to look at his bare leg. Several black worm-like creatures had attached themselves to his skin. Others of our group found we too were hosting similar organisms. Removing these bloodsuckers or leeches was neither easy nor pleasant. Suddenly the stream lost its attraction.

Attending the services provided something that couples could do together. In general, it proved to be an excellent way to encourage friendships with others outside the confines of our little valley.

Among all of the participating ministers, father's farming responsibilities were unique, requiring his returning to Brooklyn to do chores twice a day. While the distance varied based on camp location, the shortest round trip each time was twenty-five miles and in some instances much farther. Only rarely was father able to arrange for a neighbor to look after milking and caring for the stock so he could enjoy one day of meetings without interruption. In spite of this, he made a point of being present at a majority of the sessions.

While tenting was an almost universal mode, the Crowell family from Forestville had constructed a prototype of the modern motor home. Built on a truck chassis, its amenities, although crude by today's standards, were a marvel to me. Mr. Crowell had a fine sense of humor and I enjoyed talking with him as he showed me how different parts of his creation operated. Being able to sleep and cook inside and then to simply drive it all home in one piece impressed me as an excellent improvement over our equipment.

Breaking camp on the Monday following the close of the series of services was another ritual which I shared with father. Again, father insisted on helping with stacking the seats, lowering the canopy of the tabernacle, and filling in the latrine trenches before we loaded our trailer. Meanwhile mother and grandmother packed up what they could.

Saying goodbyes to friends had its element of sadness but there was always the mutual promise of "See you next camp." As high as had been the anticipation of attending camp meeting, the return to home with its familiar surroundings brought a different set of expectations. As the Chevy pulled the loaded trailer down the hill past Wings and into the valley, past the church and down the stretch of road to the parsonage, I was thinking of a warm bath in the old washtub and the comfort of my bed with a regular mattress. The lawn would need mowing and the garden was ready for attention, but all of that could wait for the morrow. Camp meeting had been great, but our valley was home.

Arbor Day
The Killing of the Trees

"Tomorrow will be Arbor Day," Miss Lincoln reminded her students just before school dismissal. "Remember that we will be going to the woods for a picnic at noon, so you'll want to bring your lunch in something easy to carry. You're dismissed." She rang the bell on her desk. Before it's note had ceased to sound, I was out of the school house door along with Don and Hank.

Arbor Day was one of those welcome diversions from the normal routine of the school day. Its legitimacy was established in New York State in 1888 by Governor David B. Hill when he signed a bill titled: "An act to encourage Arboriculture," just six years after the first recorded Arbor Day. The date chosen for its observance was the first Friday following the first day in May. The whole concept originated as an idea developed by J. Sterling Morton, an early conservationist who later served as Secretary of Agriculture in President Grover

Cleveland's cabinet. But such historical facts were not what impressed us. After a long winter, the prospect of a warm spring day away from the books and in the reawakening out-of-doors was ample cause for jubilation.

It wasn't that school was dismissed! The prescribed hours were utilized in other than routine ways. An *ARBOR DAY MANUAL* issued by the State Department of Education set forth guidelines and offered suggestions for appropriate activities. However, the specifics of its observance were left up to the individual school teachers.

As the opening activity the next morning, Miss Lincoln read a description of the giant California redwoods and how efforts were being made to save some of these magnificent trees. She followed this with a bit of history: the important role played by Johnny Appleseed in the spread of fruit trees across the United States. Making us aware of matters beyond the scope of the forested slopes of our small valley was her obvious objective.

"For our art lesson today," she explained," each one of you will cut from black paper a silhouette of a tree. Paste this on a green sheet for the background. Grading will be based on how easily I can recognize the tree from its shape." I chose to do an elm tree, as no other exhibits such a graceful vase shape.

Arbor Day would have been incomplete without the poem Carol Steinbar recited from memory - "Woodman, Spare That Tree." Lillian Woodard followed with "Trees," Joyce Kilmer's tribute to this gift to mankind. In spite of parodies by Clinton Woodard such as "Woodman, spear that tree," the words and sentiments grew familiar through repetition over the years.

"For our music today, my choice is the song by Katherine Lee Bates, 'America, the Beautiful.' If you are unsure of the words, I've written them on the blackboard." Miss Lincoln rolled up the map of the United States which had been covering her neatly printed work. Enthusiastically we joined in a resounding rendition of "O beautiful for spacious skies..."

For the students, all of this was just the prelude to the culminating activity of Arbor Day - an expedition to the woods to obtain one or more trees to plant in the school yard. The new school had been constructed on an open tract of meadow totally devoid of shrubbery of any kind. Without plantings or even a single tree to break the straight lines of the building, the impression was one of harshness. Our school would have felt right at home on the treeless prairies. There was need to visually tie the building to the land on which it stood. Arbor Day seemed like a propitious time to further this objective. We, the students, were eager to meet this challenge.

Before surrendering her charges to the freedom of the world outside the schoolhouse, Miss Lincoln carefully spelled out the subsequent schedule, replete with prohibitions. Among the latter were exhortations to not get separated in the woods and to not eat leeks. With whoops of joy, lunches and wraps in hand, the jostling bunch of children headed up the road to Pratts.

Feigning surprise, Don's Grandfather Pratt asked, "What's going on here?" The shouted responses of the students confirmed what he previously knew, as Miss Lincoln had already gotten permission to use his woods.

"May we borrow two shovels and an ax?" she asked.

"Of course you can. Don. Go fetch them."

We straggled through the barnyard, past the silent sugar house, and up the hill towards the woods. While not the orderly march of a military squad, it did assume a certain order. The older boys and girls lead the motley procession as the teacher brought up the rear, helping and encouraging the younger pupils. The warmth of the air, the chorus of the birds, and the fresh light-green of the new leaves all made it a scene of unusual charm.

"Lunchtime," the teacher called. "Find a place to sit down," she suggested.

From the grassy knoll we gazed out over the valley. The two most prominent landmarks were the school and the church. I looked for the parsonage, but the brow of the hill and a grove of maples hid it from view. Mock Hill blocked the far end of the valley. The scene was familiar, but this perspective somehow made it appear pleasingly different.

The normal fare of sandwiches constructed of home-made bread took on gourmet qualities when consumed in this setting. Some swapping always took place, prompted by curiosity and individual preferences.

"Anyone got a cookie to trade for half of a peanut butter sandwich?" Douglas Silvernail asked.

"No, but you can have half of my cake," May offered.

Carrying a beverage was too much of a hassle, so Miss Lincoln had anticipated this need by stopping at the pump in Pratt's yard. From this source came all of the water we normally used at school. The teacher had reminded everyone there would be no more to drink until we returned from the woods.

Lunch over, there were calls to "get going." Rushing from spot to spot, as someone called out a discovery, made the woods a lively place. The "finds" ranged from a little orange newt with its neat markings to a patch of Adder's Tongue blooming around the roots of a beech tree. The gray squirrels and striped chipmunks curiously regarded this noisy intrusion into their neighborhood. Drooping wildflowers - trillium, mayflowers, spring beauties, and hepaticas - whatever chose this unfortunate day to bloom - drooped and wilted in the clutch of hot grimy hands.

As the afternoon progressed, the teacher became more insistent that we find and dig up a proper tree to take back to school. Several of the older boys took turns attacking the area around a likely looking prospect. Intertwined roots and imbedded rocks spared this handsome candidate.

Finally, in desperation, we bent our efforts towards uprooting two small sugar maple saplings about an inch in diameter at the base. The shovels seemed to contact resistance at each level. By taking turns, we gradually made progress in baring the main roots. With the axe, we severed the remaining roots which attempted to maintain their hold. Sporting only the main roots devoid of any significant root hairs, the two young maples were carried triumphantly out of the woods.

We failed to report all of our discoveries to the teacher. In a moist gully Preston was attracted to fresh green leaves almost a foot high. Clair, Lillian, and I clustered around him. With eager fingers and the aid of a sharp stick we pried loose from the ground a number of their bulblets. Quickly the odor on our hands confirmed any remaining doubt. We had located a patch of leeks.

This member of the onion family grows wild in the woods, coming to new growth in May along with the spring flowers. The mild flavor of the bulbs belies the potency of their aroma on the breath. Unrealistically we somehow expected our partaking of the forbidden delicacy to be overlooked. When Miss Lincoln chose to not notice the smell, we were lulled into a false sense of security.

On the way back, the teacher halted the group to quench their thirst at the pump. Miss Lincoln requested: "Harry and Preston, bring two pails of water back to school to wet down the trees."

Then followed the interment of the unfortunate maples. I have chosen that term on purpose. We dug shallow holes in places indicated by the teacher. At least we made sure that the roots of the two maples were decently covered by soil to hide from inquisitive eyes their mutilated condition. The two pails of water baptized our flawed effort. Another Arbor Day celebration wound down as the students headed home.

As I entered our house, I expected nothing more than an observation that my clothing and hands were a bit dirtier than usual. To my surprise, mother demanded: "Arnold! Come here!" The urgency in her voice was unmistakable. I meekly complied.

"Have you been eating leeks?" she demanded.

Reeking of the evidence, my only plea was an attempt to spread responsibility.

"Preston, and Lillian, and Clair found them and gave me some." This excuse didn't succeed any better than in the Garden of Eden.

The summary verdict was: "You will stay outside until you smell fit to be with people." The final stern warning was by this time familiar to me: "Don't ever do this again."

Sitting outside on the porch steps during supper and into the evening, I had ample time to meditate on one of grandmother's aphorisms: "Sin in haste; repent at leisure."

But what of the trees? After all, they were what Arbor Day was all about. At teacher's urging, they received a few more limited outpourings of water before school let out for summer vacation. But when classes reconvened in the fall, the barbarity of their rude removal and the trauma of a long summer without water had produced the inevitable. They stood bare and leafless with their slim trunks cracked open. Zeal without knowledge had created this mockery of Arbor Day. During my attendance at District No. 6A, I don't recall that any of our Arbor Day efforts brought lasting results. Instead of enhancing their opportunity for life, we had killed the trees.

Later teachers and students may have succeeded where we

failed. As I recently drove past the old schoolhouse which has now been converted into a residence, I noted a significant number of trees gracing the lot. Maybe some subsequent Arbor Days in our valley actually lived up to their name.

If You Can't Yodel, Toot the Trumpet

As soon as I opened the parsonage door that morning on my way to school, I heard merry voices singing this hilarious ditty:

She churned the butter in her old man's boot,
Knickety, knackety, noo noo noo;
And for a dasher she stuck in her foot,
Knickety, knackity, noo, noo, noo!

Other equally amusing stanzas followed. Since only Springs and Woodards lived farther from school than I did, identifying the songsters was easy. Clinton, Clair, and Lillian soon caught up with me.

"I'd like to learn that song," I admitted shyly.

"Sing along with us," they suggested. By the time we reached the schoolhouse, I had mastered both words and tune.

Their singing was frequently accompanied by the harmonica and jew's-harp on which both Clair and Clinton were proficient.

But the ability I secretly sought to acquire was Clinton's yodeling. Sometimes he yodeled just to hear the echoes resound from the hills. On other occasions, yodeling comprised an integral part of a song he was singing. However this marvelous sound was produced, I desperately wanted to master the technique.

"Clinton. Teach me how to yodel," I begged.

"It's easy," he shrugged. "Hold your hands like this," and he cupped them in a manner I tried to duplicate.

"Now make your voice sound like this," and he produced a mellow tone. My poor imitation failed miserably, partly due to my being so self-conscious.

After school I retreated to the far corner of our pasture and tried to duplicate the haunting tones. A few doleful random squawks, my best attempts, caused our cows to stare in wonder and move cautiously away. My utter failure to master yodeling caused me to doubt my musical ability, especially when Clinton stated solicitously, "It's easy. Really nothing to it."

Although in that era the Free Methodist denomination forbade the use of musical instruments in church, the importance of singing was stressed. In fact, since instrumental accompaniment was absent, a capella singing was emphasized. Father and mother both enjoyed musical expression. Often our cows, chickens, and pigs constituted the audience as father broke into the strains of a hymn while doing the chores.

Beryl Newcomb was helping father pull a vigorous crop of thistles out of our corn field. The work was not only hot and dirty, but swarms of mosquitos were adding to their discomfort. Father started singing the chorus, "We'll work 'till Jesus comes." When father caught his breath, Beryl muttered facetiously, "Then I hope He comes soon!"

Nothing pleased father more than to have "special music" in the church service. He encouraged anyone with potential talent in this area to exercise it. Rev. Charles Pike, a retired minister who lived in Cattaraugus, was noted for his fine bass voice. Whenever he visited the Brooklyn church, invariably someone requested Hymn No. 278, "When I Can Read My Title Clear To Mansions in the Skies." In the latter part of each verse he rendered the bass solo in which words and music climaxed majestically. A burst of hearty "Amens" attested more appropriately than clapping that he had touched the hearts of the congregation. Charles Pike's talent was legendary throughout the entire Genesee Conference. Even in the large annual conference gathering, singlehanded, he was able to balance the congregation in the rendering of this powerful hymn.

In his pastoral calling, father discovered that the Higbee family had moved near East Otto village. Finding that they lacked transportation, father began to pick them up with his car on Sunday mornings. Doris, one of their daughters, was beautifully blonde and had an outstanding voice. Her solos became a frequent feature of the morning services. Although older than I and a lofty high school junior, I secretly admired her and appreciated her vocal talents.

The moving of the Baptiste family to the former Mau farm on Hammond Hill created quite a stir. They were the only black family in this all-white community. Promptly father called on them and invited them to church. Mr. Baptiste had two married daughters, one of them the mother of cute twins, Lancelot and Elaine. The twins were a hit in Sunday School with their renditions of children's songs.

But their mother and aunt produced some of the purest harmony ever heard in that little church. When they chose to sing "There is a Balm in Gilead" or "Come Ye Disconsolate," this tiny rural congregation was powerfully moved. The line from the latter hymn, "Earth hath no sorrow that Heaven cannot heal," took on special meaning. The duet became a solo the following winter when one of the sisters succumbed to pneumonia.

Special music was also provided by the George Silvernail family who lived on a farm "over west" towards Zoar. Four of their children, Clarence, Mamie, Paul, and Beatrice comprised a mixed quartet. One of their favorite selections was the gospel song, "Living For Jesus."

But singing wasn't only for those with special talents. The men of the congregation enjoyed the opportunity to periodically gather with their families for a "sing" at the parsonage. Mother played the little reed organ which had been a gift for her ninth birthday. Built in as part of the ornate woodwork of this instrument, two pedestals or lamp stands held oil lamps to illuminate the hymn book.

Most of these men were farmers who worked hard from before dawn until after dark. But, in the inspiration of singing hymns, they forgot their weariness and drudgery. Instead, their lined faces reflected joy and peace. I vividly recall the hearty involvement of Frank Reed,

Hayden Silvernail, Ward Bergholtz, and Lloyd Sprowl. When anxious wives with tired children suggested it was time to go home, Frank Reed requested: "Please, just this one more ..." And then another - and another. This plea was not from the pastor. It came from farmers who had to be up at the 3:30 am hour far preceding the winter's dawn. Some had over one hundred cows to milk by hand in time to meet the milk truck.

After the last chord from the organ had faded, those living farthest away bundled up their children, placing them under heavy blankets in the straw-lined box of the sleigh. The runners squeaked in the frozen snow as the horses broke the sleigh loose and pulled out of the parsonage yard, Bells on their harnesses jingled. The flicker of lantern light marked the exodus of others as they made their way on foot directly across the fields to their homes. They shared a song until the diverging participants drew too distant to join in the refrain. I climbed the stairs to my frigid bedroom with a warm feeling inside.

Most hymns I enjoyed. One violent exception was "Mighty Army Of the Young." My aversion came about under the following circumstances. While father was pastor at Cattaraugus, he held afternoon services at New Albion. Miss Louise Watson, unmarried and a former school teacher, was Sunday School superintendent and played the organ. Prim and stern, she announced the opening hymn for Sunday School. Invariably, Sunday after Sunday, she chose "Mighty Army Of the Young," a spirited song. My problem was that as I looked around the tiny assembly of mostly senior citizens, I saw no children except my brother, just a babe in arms, and me. Even at the age of five, the incongruity of the words in that assemblage offended my sense of appropriateness. After the passage of six decades, I still don't like to sing it.

Father's appreciation of hymns was enhanced by his exposure to Rev. D. B. Tobey. To a small boy, he was a giant of a man, well over six feet tall. His black whiskers he wore in the manner of Abraham Lincoln. His years as a lumberjack in the mountains of Western Pennsylvania prior to entering the ministry were evidenced in his impressive physique.

Father always welcomed him to our home and church. Although I don't recall much about his sermons, I still can see him seated on the platform at church, an imposing figure always garbed in black.

With eyes closed and face uplifted, he would start to sing, encouraging the congregation to join him. He sang without a book to prompt him on text or remind him of tunes. His strong voice would go on, verse after verse without any hesitation. Some of the songs he chose to sing had twenty or thirty verses. These he had committed to memory when no books were generally available in the logging camps where he preached. Indeed he was not from the present breed of song leaders who announce: "We'll sing the first, second, and last verses." This influence of D. B. Tobey with respect to hymns was reflected throughout father's ministry.

"Remember the Watch Night service Wednesday evening at the parsonage. Join us any time between eight and midnight as we welcome the New Year in with song," father exhorted his rural congregation.

Although the annual New Year's service was occasionally held at the church, often a home was chosen instead. The church was difficult to heat in winter and offered few amenities for families with small children. Too, musical instruments were forbidden. And father had lots of singing in mind when he scheduled services at our house.

When the church families gathered on New Year's Eve, father announced his ambitious plan. "Let's sing every number in "Light & Life Songs," he suggested.

"But we don't know them all," several objected.

"Then this is a fine opportunity to learn some new ones," was his reply. "Tonight we won't sing all the verses to every one," he relented. "Please turn to Number One."

In this way father kept the congregation from over-using a few numbers to the total exclusion of others. With prayer and praise interspersed, that New Year's Eve was long-remembered as "the night we sang the song book through."

"Arnold. Help me carry something in from the car." Father spoke with an uncharacteristic air of mystery.

The old Chevy had no trunk. But filling the back seat was a large bulky object. When father pulled back the old blanket protecting it, I exclaimed with delight, "A victrola!"

"It's broken," he warned. "But I think it can be fixed."

True to his word, on the next trip to Springville he brought home a new spring which restored this wondrous machine to working condition. We purchased a supply of steel needles at a cost of $.25 per hundred, as the needle required replacement after every few records. Sound was reproduced mechanically from Bakelite records. The turntable speed varied as spring tension changed, distorting the sound. Winding the crank too much risked breaking the spring or having it unhook from the spindle. In spite of its flaws, it brought a new dimension of music to the parsonage

The donor, a lady in Cattaraugus, sent along a collection of assorted records with the phonograph. Although a number of the records were scratched and worn, the group spanned a diverse spectrum of performers. Artists ranged from the Stamps-Baxter Quartet to opera with the famed Enrico Caruso and Madame Schumann- Heinck. With this limited supply, I listened over and over to all of them. Exposure to this disparate menu broadened my appreciation and enjoyment of music.

On a quiet summer evening, as dusk was falling, I heard the sweet, mellow tones of a trumpet resounding from one side of the valley to the other. Those fine sounds were produced by Gene Wing's son, Richard, home on vacation from Chesbrough Seminary. The desire to play the trumpet took mighty hold on me. But the unreality of this dream was brought clearly to me by my parents.

"Times are hard. Arnold, we just don't have money to purchase a trumpet for you," they explained sadly.

As strange as it may seem, it was the economic rigor of the era which enabled me to realize this dream. When the next annual Montgomery Ward catalog arrived, I was first to leaf through the "wish book." Just inside the cover I read words I could scarcely believe: "Young people. Earn free prizes by introducing customers to Ward's products. Send for free kit."

Rushing up to mother, I pleaded: "May I send in for it?"

She agreed reluctantly, for during the depression many dishonest schemes were spawned. She didn't want me to be disappointed. Daily I checked our mailbox. Finally the awaited packet arrived.

Along with all struggling businesses, Montgomery Ward, the catalog mail order firm, sought new ways to increase sales. Simply stated, their offer was as follows: Any person under eighteen could join the plan and receive Montgomery Ward order blanks with their name imprinted on them. By encouraging people to place orders on these special blanks, the person whose name was imprinted received a point for each dollar of goods ordered. Awards in the form of merchandise from their catalog could be earned based on the number of points accumulated. One of these premiums was a trumpet.

On my old bike I covered miles of dusty country roads, braving dogs and the suspicion of some who distrusted everyone in those discouraging times. Although very shy and self-conscious, I was driven by this dream of playing the trumpet. My hopes grew as the points started to accumulate. At church conference and camp meeting gatherings, I was on hand with my supply of order blanks. After over of year of effort, I had enough points to claim my coveted award - a trumpet which sold for $14.95 in their catalog.

Day after day I hurried home from school and on Saturdays personally met the mailman to see if my trumpet had come. When my faith had almost flickered out, one memorable day a box awaited me when I came from school. I was too excited to shout. With trembling hands I unwrapped the box and lifted the silver-plated horn with its gold bell from the bed of tissue paper in which it was nested.

Placing the shining trumpet to my lips, I blew, Not a sound came forth. I tried blowing a second time, puffing out my cheeks, and squinting my eyes with effort. Instead of a loud note of triumph, nothing happened.

A dark thought entered my mind: "Suppose this wasn't a real trumpet at all! Maybe they had sent me one that wouldn't work." Bitterly I poured out these fears to my father.

His wise response was: "Son, I think there's a bit more to playing one of these than just blowing into it. I'll see what I can find out."

True to his word, father contacted Clyde Bullock, leader of the Cattaraugus Town Band. He agreed to give me trumpet lessons once a week after he was through work. Father drove me the twelve miles to Cattaraugus and picked me up again after the half-hour lesson. The price tag for his instruction was $.25 per lesson. And I did learn to play the trumpet, in subsequent years achieving first chair in the high school band.

In his first year as band director at Cattaraugus High, where I was a freshman, Frank Gullo established his reputation as capable, dedicated, and demanding. One of his stern reminders to band members was: "As a member of this group, you don't fail alone." When the band showed remarkable improvement, he set his sights on taking us to compete in the New York State Music Festival in Endicott, almost two hundred miles away.

In preparation for this goal, Gullo insisted on additional practice sessions on Saturday mornings. At first father didn't see how he could possibly spare the time to take me the twelve miles to Cattaraugus. Mr. Gullo was adamant that only those who attended every practice could stay in the band. Father finally relented, sharing trips with other parents and organizing his activities to include calling on parishioners while I was at practice.

The first hurdle was to win over other Class D schools at Fredonia, the regional Associated Music Festival in which all bands in our area competed. The band's success there inspired community spirit, as never had a local group gone on to state competition.

On May 12, 1936, the band members and their instruments traveled in a very crowded school bus which was accompanied by Mr. Sidney Frost, the principal, driving his brand new 1936 Chevrolet. Due to the distance, staying over night was necessary. Sleeping in a hotel and eating in a restaurant were new experiences for me. The prospect both excited and intimidated me, for I didn't want to call attention to my ignorance of protocol.

Around our appearance on the program, we visited the Endicott-Johnson Shoe Works and IBM, where we were presented with Tom Watson's famous slogan - "THINK." Although we ranked second in our class in New York State, the experience marked a first breaking out of the parochialness of our little valley.

Like my idol, Richard Wing, I enjoyed playing my trumpet outdoors when the weather was warm. However, I'm not certain this great "willingness to share my talents" was always appreciated by the neighbors, especially in my earlier stages of learning.

But one magic moment stands out. Late one October afternoon I was out in the yard practicing over a number for school. The warm sun shining through the autumn haze cast a golden glow over the valley. The notes came out clear and true as the melody found its way across the fields and woods. Through the corner of my eye I caught a movement in the meadow across the road. I saw three deer standing motionless, intently listening. As the last note died away, over the fields they bounded, white tails flying like flags, until they were lost to sight in the growing dusk. Even in these bleak Depression years, music was no stranger to our rural valley.

Latch Strings and Welcome Mats

Our years of living in Brooklyn impressed on me the paradox that sharing, instead of making one poorer, actually results in enrichment. The outworking of this mysterious truth was more obvious in the realm of friendship and intangible values than in the financial and physical sense. Father and mother understood and practiced this principle as they "cast their bread upon the waters."

The Brooklyn parsonage was modest in size - really no larger than necessary to accommodate our immediate family. Even the wide hallway at the top of the stairs had to serve as grandmother's bedroom. Irving and I shared a small bedroom where the ceiling slanted down due to the slope of the roof. And yet my parents made room to share.

Because of the loss of his job due to the Depression, Ephraim Vail, a life-long friend of my parents, was forced to search for work wherever it could be found. An expert electrician and mechanic, he located a position in Jersey City, far from his Akron home. During this period of his absence in the winter of 1929-30 and at other times, his wife Lillian and daughter Grace came to live with us. I'm sure some benefits were reciprocal. I truly believe there was nothing mechanical or electrical that Ephie Vail couldn't fix. His ministrations to the old Chevy at one time or another spanned everything from a carburetor adjustment to a total engine overhaul.

Holiday times were very special as he returned from Jersey City to visit his family at the parsonage. The Christmas of 1930 stands out, for he brought us a bag of chestnuts. The blight had killed most of the native chestnut trees, so I missed the pleasure of picking them up as I had done in our yard in Belfast. We roasted them over the fire in the kitchen range. "Aunt" Lillian put together a special kind of cookie containing dates, coconut, and walnuts, ingredients which Ephie had acquired in the city.

Although several years younger than I, in some ways, Grace acted like the sister I never had. Some of the time her brother Roy also lived at the parsonage. He was too worldly-wise for his years and irritated me by acting superior. Otherwise, the arrangement worked out well for us to live as an extended family.

"Grandma Silvernail wants to stay with us for the winter," father announced one fall morning. Mother had apparently agreed to her coming. I was less enthusiastic about this news.

This second sharing of our home left me with far different feelings. Grandma Silvernail had several married children with whom she rotated her time. However, during several winters, she came to stay at our house. Because of age and infirmity which made climbing stairs difficult, my parents gave up for her the only downstairs bedroom and moved to the unheated upstairs room. A serious problem developed.

"Arnold, you're holding the book too near your eyes."

"Why don't you go out and shovel the walk?"

"It's getting cool in here. Check the stove."

"Do you and Irving need to be so noisy? Why don't you go outside and play!"

I resented her ordering me around. "Please" was not in her vocabulary. Her manner to my parents was all sweetness. With two other women in the house, my own grandmother and mother, I strongly resented her intrusion into my life. Her constant presence, sitting in my grandmother's favorite rocking chair next to the Round Oak heater, caused me to avoid her as much as possible by finding things to do outside. No family matters escaped her sharp ears. My complaints to mother were answered with her kindly, "But she's old and needs our help." Her departure in the spring was for me a cause of rejoicing.

Short-term guests were a regular happening which brought variety and interest to our rural existence. Four times yearly, Rev. Wesley Parmerter, the district superintendent, came for services. On several of these weekends, he brought his wife and children, Stan and Jean, my friends from camp meeting. Each time I looked forward to sharing with these two red-headed friends my special places along the creek and in the woods. A succession of missionaries, evangelists, and special speakers were welcomed to the pastor's home. I do not know how mother managed to handle accommodations for everyone.

Our dinner table, especially on Sunday noons, was frequently expanded beyond our immediate family. Putting additional leaves in the table to extend it was one of my ways of assisting. With grandmother's help, mother usually had the potatoes peeled and vegetables prepared and soaking in water before leaving for church. Since we had to depart about 9:30 to make Sunday School on time and didn't get home until nearly one, leaving anything cooking on the wood range was impractical.

With the revised number for dinner known, mother peeled more potatoes. She had mastered the art of making resources stretch. Even the old colonel of Kentucky Fried Chicken fame could have learned a thing or two from mother about how many portions of meat could be derived from a given cut. Sometimes my heart sank as I observed the shrinkage in the wedge size of the apple pie. But, if anyone received a short portion, it was mother - and no one else was made aware of her sacrifice.

Company at any time was always welcome. Advance notice or formal invitations were never needed or expected. This practice never changed throughout my parents' lives. I believe there were several reasons why people were attracted to our home. Foremost was the genuine interest they took in people and their problems. This went beyond a pastor and his wife performing as professionals in the line of duty. They both genuinely liked people and knew how to express this in practical ways. I believe that Grace Vail Pratt caught the spirit of our home in her comment: "People liked to come there because it was a happy place."

In spite of the primitive implements with which to work, mother made sure the house was clean. She did not believe that worn linoleum excused dirty linoleum. Her penchant for cleanliness brought me one of my most disliked household tasks - beating the carpets. The hand-propelled carpet sweeper was used regularly, but dirt still accumulated in the fibers of the living room carpet. Bringing in wood and carrying out ashes contributed to this undesired buildup.

When father and mother had carried the worn carpet outside and hung it over the clothesline in the front yard, mother handed me the carpet beater.

"Arnold, do a good job. Beat it all over both front and back. I want to check it when you're finished." Mother believed in quality control through inspection.

Holding by its wooden handle this instrument for the torture of carpets and boys, I struck the rug a blow with the wire grid. A puff of dust filled the air. Again and again I wielded the beater. I choked and sneezed as dust particles irritated my nose and throat. My dislike for the job added to my vigor as I took out my aggressions on the helpless carpet.

"Mother!" I called. "Come and check it now?"

Her sharp eyes examined one side and then the other. "Give it a few more strokes on this corner," she said, pointing.

Finally released from this periodic ceremony of house cleaning, I was aware that cleanliness had its price.

Every house into which we ever moved needed to be painted and to have fresh paper hung on the walls and ceilings. Brooklyn parsonage was no exception. Fortunately father enjoyed painting and, through practice, he became an expert paper-hanger. He purchased most of our wallpaper by mail from Robinson's Golden Rule factory in Titusville, Pennsylvania. With wallpaper selling for only five or ten cents per roll, father could see no excuse for loose, smoke-grimed paper on our walls. His skills became so well known that area residents hired him to do papering and painting for them. While time-consuming, this added to our family income, although he never charged going prices for his work.

Mother skillfully assisted father in the paper hanging by pasting the long strips and trimming them. My parents worked efficiently as a team. When a papering job came up on a Saturday or during vacation, I was sometimes pressed into service. Wielding the drippy paste brush in a way to thoroughly cover the back of the paper without smearing it on the good side did not come naturally to me. Father's disappointment at my lack of finesse made for some tense moments, especially when it affected the finished result in someone else's home.

"Arnold. you're dripping paste over the edges."

"Spread the paste out evenly. This strip has dry spots and will never stick."

"This border isn't trimmed evenly. Hand me the shears."

Father was a perfectionist. Our mutual experiences hanging paper carried little satisfaction for either of us. Since my son and daughter skillfully practice this art, I have developed a theory that paperhanging and painting skills skip a generation. My ineptness in paperhanging I present as proof of this theory.

Father and mother thought that home should look attractive on the outside. When some vigorous work could change things, they could see no reason for a cluttered and overgrown yard. Here the major tool was a push-type reel lawn mower. Of all of the outside work, mowing lawn was my favorite. To get the surface extra smooth, I often mowed it twice. Father thought that degree of manicure not really necessary.

"You've been over that enough," he suggested. "I can find you something more profitable to take your time."

I liked to make it as velvety as possible to improve the surface for the croquet games we played. All of the family except for father avidly participated. Grandmother's love of flowers exhibited itself in colorful borders along the walk and touches of color around the old stone foundation. Zinnias, cosmos, cockscomb, and portulaca were some of her favorites.

Father and mother never let the lack of amenities such as indoor plumbing, running water, and electricity act as deterrents to welcoming people, regardless of their background. They simply let the genuineness of their hospitality compensate for what they could not offer in physical facilities. And this attitude was effective. For, as the years pass, I continue to encounter people whose lives were affected permanently by their exposure, brief or lengthy, to the parsonage in Brooklyn valley.

The strength of this influence may have stemmed from what appears to have been the opposite impression too often exhibited by Christians. On a November Sunday evening in 1946, I arrived in Chicago after an all-day train trip from Batavia, New York. I was enrolled for a course in refrigeration at a technical institute which was supposed to provide housing. When I reached the designated address, I was told all of its rooms were filled. I would have to fend for myself. Phone calls to hotels turned up nothing, as it was still a period when only servicemen were accepted for the limited accommodations.

Near my intended lodging I had noticed from the taxicab window a lighted church with a banner announcing that Vance Havner was to speak in the evening service. In desperation, I picked up my suitcase and walked to the church through the gathering dusk. Sharp gusts of wind drove the mixture of rain and sleet into my face, proclaiming that late November in Chicago was not a season to spend the night without shelter.

A smiling usher, fashionably attired with a rose in his lapel, greeted me at the door. The Gideon emblem which he also displayed encouraged me to share with him my plight, as I too belonged to that organization. He assured me he would talk with the pastor and others and see what he could do. Vance Havner was his usual inimitable self in his unique presentation of the gospel. A warm glow enveloped the congregation.

After dismissal, I waited at the spot indicated for the usher to reappear. His response was that no one in that large evangelical church had room to house one stranded young man for the night. Although a providential solution appeared from a totally different source, I couldn't help but contemplate the contrast between my reception and that which would have been accorded a stranger had he come to the little white church in the Brooklyn valley.

Bees and Bears, Serpents and Grasshoppers

One sweltering July afternoon, mother went to the door to see who was knocking.

"G'afternoon, Miz Cook," greeted Harriet Wing. "I'm a bit tuckered out with the heat. Mind if I set a spell?"

"With a batch of bread in the oven, it's too hot to stay inside. Why don't we sit out here on the porch?" mother suggested.

Mrs. Wing settled her ample girth on the shady bench, shielded from the road by rampant morning glory vines which Grandma Willis had trained to cling to a string trellis running to the roof of the porch. Hearing the conversation, grandma appeared to join them in her rocker. From a shady spot under our big elm where I had been target practicing with my slingshot, I had observed Harriet Wing's approach.

Willie Wing's mother and father, Sylvester and Harriet, lived in a rude two-room cabin back in the woods about a mile from the parsonage. According to reliable reports of our neighbors, they customarily sat, one on each side of a hole cut in the floor of the main room. Both found pleasure in chewing tobacco. As they chewed, they vied with each other in projecting the juicy discharge through the hole. This arrangement eliminated the need for emptying a spittoon.

Having become aware in the past of Mrs. Wing's entertaining accounts of local people and events, I ambled across the road and sat in the shade, my back up against the porch railing. I kept busy whittling on the handle of my slingshot as the women made conversation about the weather, prospects for the blackberry crop, and current happenings in the valley. I waited some minutes for a lull in the conversation. Harriet found the attention of an interested audience very satisfying and required only a "Yes" or a question from her hearers to reassure her they were listening.

At the first opportune pause, I requested: "Please tell about the big snake." Obviously I had heard the tale before, but I enjoyed it so much that repetition tantalized my imagination. She needed no urging and launched at once into her graphic account.

"I was pickin' red razzberries and black caps along the crick up towards the old Garlock place. It was hot and I wuz tuckered out with climbin' up and down the banks where the best berries grow. I decided to go to a cool spot along the crick on a shady ledge just above "rockbottom" with its little falls. Seein' a big log, I put my half-full pail of berries on the ground and set down on the log. It looked a little funny, but I didn't think much about it.

"I wuz thinkin' about how tired and sweaty I wuz and wunderin' whether to pick more berries or go home to the cabin. Sudden-like the log seemed to stir. First-off I thought it must be an earthquake. Then I noticed the log wuz movin' but the earth was standin' still. I saw the "log" didn't have bark at all. It looked all scaly-like. Sudden-like it cum to me. I'd been settin' on a huge serpent.

"I wuz skeered out of my mind. I fergot my pail of berries and took out through the woods straight for the cabin. I never even looked back or stopped runnin' til I got home. Lucky I wuz that Sylvester wuz there."

"'What's the matter with you, woman?' he asked. 'You look like you seen a ghost.'

"Soon's I could ketch my breath, I told him about the huge snake by the crick. He grabbed his gun and took the dog, headin' to the place which he reconized when I told him. 'Bout an hour later he cum back, carryin' my pail of berries. 'Couldn't find nothin' a'tall,' he grunted. 'Clumb up and down both sides of the crick and the hound never hit a scent.'

"S'the truth, so help me. There's things down in them woods that a body ought to watch out fer. I'm feelin' better now, so I'll be headin' home. Thanks for lettin' me set and talk."

Soon she was out of sight, cutting across the fields beyond Brooklyn Bridge to her cabin in the woods. One effect of this story on my behavior for a long time afterwards was that I carefully looked at any log before I sat on it.

* * * * *

On my way home from school, I heard someone singing. When I reached the little bridge over the west tributary of the creek, I was sure the singer was John Nelligan who lived in the second house west of the parsonage. My conclusion was confirmed as I caught the words in the chorus of John's favorite gospel song:

"I'll away, I'll away to the Promised Land.
I'll away, I'll away to the Promised Land.
When my Father calls me I will go,
To meet Him in the Promised Land."

John Nelligan was a small man, both thin and short of stature. His wife, Caroline, was a "fleshy" lady. She had cancer and spent much of her time in bed or propped up on pillows in a chair. With some frequency, John appeared at our door either day or night with the news that his wife was dying.

"Parson, would you come and pray with Caroline?" was his standard request. In spite of the frequency of this recurrence, father always obliged. Because of the care she required, John seldom was able to attend church, but he and his wife welcomed having a cottage prayer meeting held in their home. Each time he requested the singing of "I'll away to the Promised Land." In his peculiar German brogue, he made the refrain ring out lustily.

As I approached his house, the sound of his ax chopping wood mingled with the tones of the song. As soon as he saw me, he called out, "Hi there, sonny."

"Hello, Mr. Nelligan," I responded.

As he often had interesting stories to tell, occasionally I halted to chat a little. Only my chores awaited me when I got home and they could wait. Father always took time to stop and talk with people, so I reasoned that he was not apt to criticize me for doing the same thing. I sauntered over to where Mr. Nelligan was standing at the wood pile.

John's right thumb was gnarled and crooked, tilting off in an odd direction at the first joint. He noticed that I was staring at it. Suddenly he asked, "Do you want to know how my thumb cum to be like this?"

"Of course I do" was my response. This was the account he gave.

"One day in August my brother and me wuz lookin' fer somethin' to do. We wuz about six and eight years old. I seed some whoppin' grasshoppers jumpin' and flyin' through the air.

"'Let's catch some grasshoppers,' I suggested. They wuz really big ones. Soon our hands wuz covered with brown stuff which they give off. We called it 'tobacco spit.'

"My brother said, 'Let's chop off their heads with the ax.'

"We took turns. He would hold the grasshopper on the choppin' block and I would chop his head off. The next time I would hold and he would chop. We wuz havin' fun. Then it wuz my turn to hold. I don't know whether I moved my hand or if my brother miscalculated the blow. I felt a sharp pain and saw the end of my thumb lyin' on the choppin' block next to the grasshopper's head.

"We wuz both shocked. Instinctive-like I grabbed up the end of my thumb and held it against the stub. If my mother found out, I knew I wuz in for a strappin'. Then I thought of the cobbler who had his shop next door at one side of his house. I run pell mell over there, holdin' the two pieces together.

"Please fasten my thumb back together', I begged.

"Acting quickly, he told me to hold the end of my thumb tight in place against the stump. Then he took some hot tallow and beeswax from a little pot he kept heated to put on the seams of shoes to seal 'em. Then he wound some sturdy cloth tight around it and tied it with shoemaker's heavy thread.

"'Leave that on for two or three weeks,' he told me. 'If it don't get infected, it might heal.'

"Sure enough, it did heal back together. Feel that lump."

I gingerly touched the point where the end of the thumb angled off. Sure enough, I felt a hard lump of some sort under the skin.

"That's a lump of that tallow in there which proves it's the truth I'm telling," concluded John Nelligan.

In spite of the improbability of this "miracle," John Nelligan was unwavering in his assertions of what had happened that August day so long ago. When I went on home, I told my mother the story of the severed thumb. Her only comment was, "Don't you ever try that!"

* * * * *

"Willie Wing's going around to the back door. Elmer, go see what he wants," grandma urged my father.

Willie Wing lived in a little shanty by the creek half way between our house and the church. What regular work he did was as hired man on the Pratt farm. His first preference was for those activities connected with the out-of-doors. During coon season, the baying of his hounds echoed regularly from the hillsides on the night air. While not the paragon of the "Protestant work ethic," he demonstrated his generosity time and again. If he experienced good luck fishing all night at the Cattaraugus Creek, he appeared at the parsonage the next morning with a string of bullheads or suckers. Willie's knowledge of the local woods and their inhabitants far surpassed that of anyone else in the community.

On his jaunts through the hills, it was not surprising that he located bee trees: hollow trunks where wild bees had deposited the sweet essence of their summer labor. Local custom was observed that whoever found a bee tree could lay claim to it by carving his initials on the trunk. It was usual courtesy to inform the owner of the land where it stood before going to collect this stored treasure.

Willie and a few others had developed the ability to locate bee trees by "lining." Placing some honey or sugar water in a jar, he would attract a bee. After keeping it confined for a short time, he then would open the jar and let the bee fly away. His keen eyesight permitted him to follow the flight of the bee as it headed "home" in a straight line. In this way, the bee would literally lead him to the honey tree. From this phenomenon of nature was derived the term "making a bee line." Willie took mental note of his discoveries for later extraction.

On the previous night, armed with saw and ax, Willie had felled a bee tree. Breaking open the trunk, he had scooped out the sticky hoard. I had followed father out to the back door, but stayed in the shelter of the shed. I was fascinated that anyone could cope so fearlessly with those stinging creatures. My personal encounters with bees, wasps, hornets, and yellow-jackets had always ended in fiery pain and subsequent discomfort with swelling from the bites. The time I walked right over a yellow-jackets' nest in the potato patch, I emerged speedily, but not before two dozen of the little rascals had made intimate contact. I viewed with awe Willie's ability to ignore the stinging bees. Some attributed this apparent immunity to the infrequency of his bathing.

"Cut a bee tree last night," Willie informed father. "Could you use some honey?"

"Certainly could," father responded quickly. Father's preference for honey ranked even above his taste for maple syrup.

"Get a dishpan," Willie suggested.

Bringing one from the kitchen, I proceeded cautiously, as several obviously angry bees had followed their trove of treasure all the way from the woods. There, in a small washtub, I viewed the sticky, golden mass. But it looked more like a diamond in the rough. Slivers of wood and dead bees were mixed through the ruptured honeycomb.

With a wooden paddle, Willie transferred a generous portion of the amber sweetness to the pan I was holding. Later, mother extracted and strained the honey which father favored on top of homemade buckwheat pancakes. Sharing a part of his good fortune came naturally to this kind-hearted man.

* * * * *

Even generosity can bring trouble to the donor. Willie Wing discovered this to his sorrow late one fall. It came about in this manner.

Looking out of the window near his desk, Eddie Spring's eyes bugged out. Poking Clair Woodard, who sat ahead of him, he pointed out of the window. Ambling past the old schoolhouse of East Otto District 6A was a black bear. They snatched a few more glimpses of the furry wanderer before he lumbered through the Hintz property and disappeared into the trees along the creek.

A bit later Willie left his humble abode to check on his traps. Muskrats were his most prevalent quarry, augmented by skunk and a rare mink. Acquired knowledge of animal behavior brought him a modest return through the sale of pelts. Willie always carried a gun on these rounds - on this particular day it was his trusty twelve gauge double-barreled shotgun. His pockets held a supply of shells - loaded with birdshot. Racing ahead and sniffing out the territory was a hound dog, his constant companion on these forays.

Checking the various sets along the creek bank brought Willie to the spot where the two small streams joined forces behind the parsonage. After resetting a sprung trap, he was pushing his way through a thicket when his hound began to sound out. The call indicated that the dog had treed something. Expecting a coon or possum, Willie burst upon the scene to find the hound barking at the foot of a big hemlock. Looking up, he saw a black bear clinging to the limbs about ten feet above the snowy ground. Calling off the dog and going on his way never occurred to Willie. Although bears were not common in the valley, there was a listed open season for hunting them.

Willie slipped two shells into his shotgun, took aim, and fired one barrel, then the other. Birdshot to a bear was more of an indignity than a life-threatening assault. Before Willie could reload, the angry bear hurtled down the tree, clawing at the surprised hound. With understandable rage, he then headed towards Willie, his tormentor.

Willie decided to put some distance between himself and the bear by climbing a tree. Hanging onto his gun, this was no easy matter. But black bears too are very good climbers in spite of their size and apparent clumsiness. Their sharp claws easily grip the tree trunk. Seeing the bear climbing up the same tree sent Willie struggling even higher. But the bear moved up too. The excited hound exploded with a frenzy of baying as it danced around the foot of the tree.

Willie searched in his pockets again, but came up with only more birdshot shells. He loaded quickly and fired two more charges directly down at the bear's head. Growling in pain and fury, up the tree the bear progressed. Willie jammed one more set of shells into the gun as the bear's claws tore into the bark just below his feet.

Partially blinded by the previous charge, the bear couldn't see clearly, but it smelled its prey, not an unusual feat considering who it was. Knowing he was no match for the sharp claws, just as the bear opened his big jaws in a snarl of fury, Willie jammed the gun barrel right into the gaping red mouth and pulled both triggers.

The recoil nearly dislodged Willie's grip on the limb. Suddenly the upward momentum of the bear stopped, gradually reversed, and with a splintering of limbs its bulky body fell to the ground with a heavy thud.

Willie's nephew, Ray, had heard the dog's frenzied yelping from where he had been tending his own trap line. Hurrying to the scene, he found Willie still up the tree and the mortally wounded bear still thrashing on the ground. A very relieved Willie clambered down the tree.

After dressing out the bear and removing the pelt, Ray and Willie carried this trophy back to their cabin. There they hung the meat in a tree to keep cool. Then Willie got the idea of sharing the bear meat with his neighbors. This he proceeded to do, doling out chunks of this exotic animal to the homes around the valley.

Then a miscalculation of timing entered the picture. The open season on bear had expired the day before he bagged his trophy. Because Willie could neither read nor write, he kept track of months and days by cutting notches in a stick. Apparently he had forgotten to cut a notch for one day and this had thrown his "calendar" off.

Willie was never one to keep his exploits secret. Word spread many directions in the county and reached the game warden. To everyone's surprise, this enforcer of the law appeared in the valley. He readily learned from Willie the names of the donees to whom he had given the bear meat. Typical was the scene at the Woodard farmhouse. Finding bear meat cooking on the stove, the warden seized it in the name of the law. The accumulated supply he transported to Machias where it made a meal for the residents of the county home.

Willie was hauled into court where the Justice of the Peace levied a fine of $25.00 for his violation of the hunting laws. Each family to whom he had given a part of the bear was fined $12.50. With the going rate of pay for a farm laborer in the range of seventy-five cents to a dollar per day, the magnitude of the fines was substantial.

Since it was early in the trapping season, Willie had no money to offer. Although Frank Woodard had his own fine to pay, he borrowed money and paid Willie's assessment so this simple, generous fellow wouldn't have to go to jail. And Willie repaid the advance through the sale of pelts before winter was over.

Outrage at the high-handed actions of the game warden rumbled through the valley for some time afterwards. If any morals can be gleaned from this true account they might be as follows: Don't count on your bear stew until it is safely in your stomach. And don't hunt big game with a BB gun.

For a simple man, one who in all of his life had scarcely been outside the immediate area of his birth, Willie Wing's obituary was unusually long, totaling fifty column lines in the newspaper. What was printed about him was even more remarkable. Here is just a segment of that account which appeared in "THE CATTARAUGUS TIMES:"

> Mr. Wing was a great lover of nature, fond of hunting, fishing and trapping. The family home had been located in the forest during the early part of his life. He had lived on Mock Hill, and for the past several years in Brooklyn. He had taken care of his father and mother. He was a good neighbor and will be missed.
>
> . . . . .
>
> The present generation is too often content to bask in the light and achievements and virtues of their forefathers without acquiring the virtues themselves. But Mr. Wing was not of this order and was an improvement on his ancestors. A more fitting epitaph could not be devised than, 'Here Lies an Honest Man.'

"What's Out There?"

The ring of hills defining the Brooklyn valley limited the vistas visible to my eyes. Unlike Willie Wing, I was not content to permit the perimeter of the valley to determine the boundaries of my life. Instead, a variety of influences and incidents conspired to broaden my horizons. This process partially accounts for the person I have become.

My addiction to books began in earnest in the little one-room district school. Limitations in its collection forced me to explore volumes on topics I would probably not have chosen if more "appropriate" titles had been available. Through reading, I entered so completely into the scenes and experiences flowing from the pages of books that, on occasion, I failed to hear the teacher announce recitation time for my class.

"Arnold, would you care to join the class today?" the teacher spoke partly in jest. Blushing in embarrassment, I put away the book in which I had been so engrossed and hurried to the front where my class had been called to recite.

My parents subscribed to "THE DAILY NEWS" from Batavia, New York, their home area. I gleaned information about what was happening currently in the national and world scene. Thus began my habit of keeping up with current events.

One of the two comic strips carried by this daily was Scorchy Smith. The exploits of this daring young man sparked my interest in the American West. Surrounded by several big rattlers in a Rocky Mountain canyon, he had only one bullet left in his pistol. With unerring calculation, the shot ricochetted from rock to rock, in the process killing all of the menacing serpents. Scorchy wore knee-length leather boots with a special little pocket to hold his jack-knife. At that point in time, more than anything else, I wanted to own a pair of boots like Scorchy's. Had a genie magically produced them, I could not have pulled them on over my twisted feet, for my arches did not bend. But the lure of the West was lodged firmly in my thoughts.

For a birthday present, my parents gave me a year's subscription to a young people's magazine. I eagerly watched for it to arrive weekly in the mail box. The stories and articles further fired my imagination.

When a short story contest was announced by the magazine, I decided to write a story about the west. From a Colorado map at school, I chose the intriguing town of Cripple Creek as the setting for my tale. The story centered around some teenagers who, through resourceful action, survived a blizzard. My parents were even more amazed than I when my entry received first prize and the paper printed my story. The First Prize in this national contest was $5.00. These were Depression days.

When father went to call on the Booths, I was more than willing to accompany him. They had a complete collection of the Horatio Alger books which they lent me. I perused every one. Each of them had essentially the same plot of poor boy works hard under overwhelming odds, only to have ultimate success crown his heroic efforts. Not only were they a tribute to the Protestant Work Ethic; in addition, the graphic descriptions of far-away places and exotic settings increased my longing to see things beyond our valley.

A by-product of parsonage hospitality had a profound influence on my perspective. Missionaries, educators, church leaders, and a broad spectrum of cultured people who visited our home helped me to see beyond the norms of the community. The China of the Schlossers, Lawrence Arksey's Africa, and the India illuminated by the Roots all expanded my world.

Each time I succeeded in getting Ephraim Vail to talk about his auto trip to the west coast and back in 1926, I paid attention to every detail. Word pictures of the United States, Africa, India, China, Japan, and Central America took the place of the modern video or slide show. To these guests in our home, I posed many questions. For me, this personal interchange provided a dimension of reality superior to that offered by the printed page.

"Pastor, would you care to bring the family to our place tomorrow night? I think you'd like to hear the special program from Churchill Tabernacle." Lloyd Sprowl, my friend Don's father, had just purchased a battery-operated radio and wanted to share it with us.

When father agreed to accept the invitation, I could scarcely wait to hear this communication marvel. We arrived well before the time of the scheduled program. Don's mother arranged all of us in a semi-circle around the speaker. Absolute silence was demanded to understand the crackling sounds which emanated from the big conical speaker.

Pratts and Sprowls became regular listeners to the broadcasts from Churchill Tabernacle in Buffalo which pronounced itself to be "Buffalo's Largest Spiritual Workshop." The all-night services from the tabernacle on New Year's Eve featured the greats of gospel music of whom Homer Rodeheaver was then chief. Local and national groups such as the Cleveland Colored Quintet and the Claus Family Singers from the Tonawanda Indian Reservation alternated numbers with the hundred voice white-robed choir. The cost of batteries, short-lived in those days, dictated group rather than individual listening. One exception was the Gene Wing household where their Atwater-Kent radio was powered by a Delco electric generating system.

After this exposure to long-distance listening, I made father aware of how much I wanted a radio. The day he brought home a battery set, my joy knew no bounds. Someone had given it to father because it wasn't working and they had purchased a new one. He took it to a man named Ellsworth at East Otto to have it fixed. That was the last I saw of it. Before the needed tubes arrived, his shop burned and our radio with it.

When several pupils in our district school simultaneously were in the eighth grade, an arrangement was made for us to attend East Otto Union School in the village three miles distant. No bus transportation was provided. Getting to and from school was the responsibility of our parents. Since this change was made in midwinter, various parents tried to coordinate their trips to town around the school schedule.

The vehicles in which we rode to school varied in their amenities. Carl Spring, whose son Ed was in the group, had an old Chevy coupe with a rumble seat. With the wind in our faces on a pleasant day, riding in the rumble seat was a lark. On a zero day or when rain and sleet beat into our faces, the trip was almost unbearable even when we huddled under a blanket. In desperation, we sometimes crammed ourselves down into the cramped compartment and pulled the door shut over our heads. This was like riding all folded up in the closed trunk of a car. When communication broke down and no one showed up, we trudged the three miles home. How glad we were when spring returned! Then we enjoyed the independence of riding our bikes to and from school.

I found greater challenge in attending a school where teachers had limited subject responsibilities and more expertise in their areas. Music instruction plus the availability of courses not offered in district school provided breadth and opened to me new areas of interest.

One positive consequence of taking Agriculture One was confirmation of what probably has become apparent: I didn't want to ever be a dairy farmer. The prospect of learning a foreign language and the stirring up of an interest in literature were stimuli from that year. Although the enrollment at East Otto Union School was relatively small, attending there did offer a widening of my acquaintance with other young people and influenced my social development.

The fall of 1935 brought a dramatic change to my educational opportunities. School bus transportation for high school students was voted by our district. I still recall the excitement of that first morning as I awaited the arrival of the bus to take us to Cattaraugus High, twelve miles away. I lived almost at the end of the run; only Springs and Woodards lived beyond us. Consequently I was one of the first to be picked up in the morning and last to arrive home.

Many firsts assailed me on that opening day: new homeroom, new locker, new teachers, new classmates, and new subjects. To top it off, I joined the high school band. Truly the world beckoned in an exciting way! Learning so many new things acted as a potent stimulant to faithful study. Even study hall I enjoyed, for Chloe Longley was reputed to have rear-view vision. Her study halls provided the orderly environment which suited me.

The winter of 1935 was noteworthy for the unusually heavy snowfalls which closed the roads for days at a time. On several days our school bus was unable to reach the valley. Students on back roads were carried by horse-drawn sleighs out to points which the school bus had succeeded in reaching. Even the mail trucks were unable to get through the big drifts. One Sunday father canceled services at Brooklyn Church due to the deeply-drifted snow - a most unusual occurrence!

Riding the bus turned from a joy into psychological trauma. While the long trip over rough roads under poor weather conditions wasn't always comfortable, that was the least of my problems. My self-consciousness around girls somehow became known to the other students on the bus. However I tried to avoid sitting with a girl, others on the bus contrived to defeat my cleverest strategies. The girls seemed to enjoy my discomfiture as much as the fellows. As I attempted to change seats while the bus was in motion, the bus driver, Mr. Mosher, reprimanded me. This really crushed me, as it happened in front of the full bus. Although I still do not look back on that year of bus riding with much pleasure, it forced me out of my shell socially as well as educationally.

I began to think about college, which would mean leaving the valley.

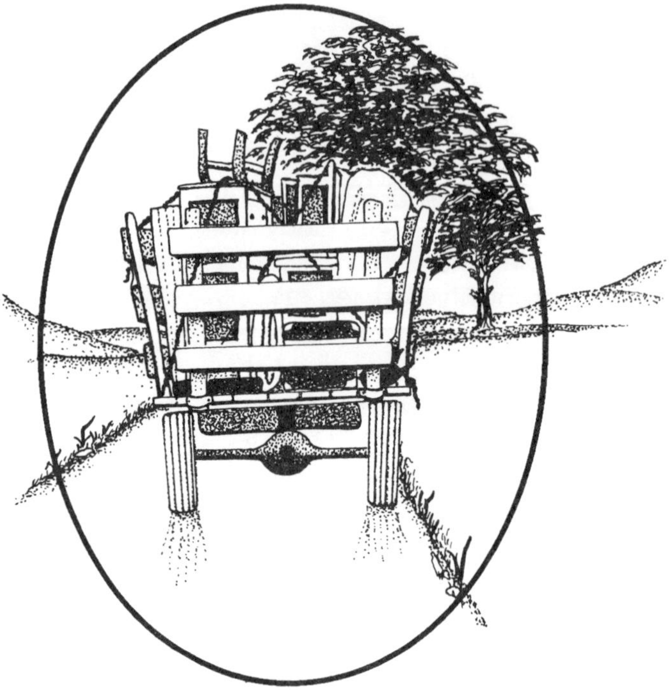

Legacy of the Valley

The annual meeting of the Genesee Conference was sometimes held in North Chili at A. M. Chesbro Seminary (Now Roberts Wesleyan College). On several occasions I accompanied my parents to this gathering. Mother was an alumna and they hoped to interest me in attending.

One significant tie connected this educational institution near Rochester with Brooklyn valley. On February 22, 1877, George W. Garlock, president of Chesbro from 1921-31, was born in a little cabin up on the hill behind the parsonage. He lived there with his father and mother, Fremont and Jennie Garlock, and four sisters, Libby, Dora, Bessie, and Flora. In 1898 the family moved to Tuna Creek, north of Bradford, Pennsylvania. No doubt he received his grade school education at old School District No. 6A, the same one I attended.

I crossed the creek behind the parsonage and climbed the hill to again locate the site of the Garlock cabin. Some rocks from the foundation still outlined where the structure had stood. No other obvious evidence of the building remained. Even the location of the dirt road which had lead down into the valley was almost obliterated. The most visible surviving feature of the Garlock homestead was a small apple orchard. The trees were overgrown and untended. I filled the pockets of my jacket with a few of the red apples which had fallen to the ground. I thought about this local boy who had distinguished himself in the area of education. Could I not follow the example of George Garlock who had preceded me out of the valley by almost half a century? Again my aspirations rose beyond the valley.

* * * * *

Alert, I watched the road and listened for the sound of our car. My parents had been attending annual conference in early September of 1936. The rumors circulating made me aware that a change for us was in the air. With school beginning on Tuesday, I worried about where we might be moved and how this would delay my start, wherever it might be. Besides, I was ambivalent, torn between anticipation of possible change and fearing the severing of ties of friendship which bound us to the people of Brooklyn Valley. At that time, nine of my thirteen years had been spent in this vale of my birth.

My ears caught the sound of a motor which could belong to none other than our old Chevy. Before father could even turn off the ignition, I had my foot on the running board. That mother and father were both smiling seemed a good omen.

"Are we moving? Where to? How soon do we leave?" My eager questions tumbled out in quick succession.

"I've been appointed to Gowanda," father answered. "I hope we can be moved by the end of the week. That depends on when we can get a truck to take our things."

This timetable for moving made for fast transition. The pastoral changes normally took place quickly so the Sunday immediately following conference found the pastors in their new pulpits. The new school term starting the day after Labor Day injected a sense of urgency in getting the families moved.

Word traveled quickly in this small community. When our Chevy drove into Pratt's yard on Friday night, the yard was full of people and vehicles. All of the downstairs was lit up. The major activities were focused in the kitchen and dining room. A genuine outpouring of goodwill and appreciation for my parents came in the form of both words and deeds. I was so excited with saying "Good-bye" to my friends, especially Don, that the tears of sadness on so many cheeks didn't register with me until later.

By the time they called on father for grace before eating, the tables almost groaned beneath their burden. Represented there were examples of the best desserts the housewives could devise. In my unofficial judging, the butternut cake easily took first prize. Lula Sprowl not only decorated the thick brown frosting with butternut kernels but also ground up some nuts to mix in the batter.

Father assured his flock that the conference was sending them a full-time pastor or otherwise he would not have ended his term as conference missionary to their church. He described the new appointee, Rev. Wallace B. Newcomb, as "a fine young man, unmarried, but one who understood farming and farmers, as he had attended Cornell University." Father's extra-long benediction brought a lump even to my throat. That we were actually leaving suddenly became very real.

By the time the truck arrived on Saturday to transport the majority of our household goods, I could scarcely contain myself. This was not Mayflower or Bekins! Two or three men from the church helped father pile our belongings on George Fleckenstein's milk truck which he had equipped with stake racks.

At each move, mother always wondered what permanent marks would be impressed into the wood surface of some articles of furniture to commemorate the transfer. It always happened. The only question was which of the chairs, tables, or bedsteads would bear the scars. In a sense, these inadvertent "carvings" conserved history much as did the totem poles in the Pacific Northwest.

On this trip to Gowanda, Edwin Fleckenstein, who was driving his brother's truck, looked in the rear-view mirror. To his surprise, he saw grandma's favorite rocking chair back in the road. It was upright, rocking back and forth in the breeze. Stopping the truck, Edwin rushed back and retrieved it, relieved to discover that only minor scratches gave a clue to its near-destruction.

Sometimes strange incidents took place in the moving process. It was common practice to reduce the cost by having the same truck unload the new pastor's goods and pick up those of the departing clergyman. As the opposite flows of furniture became mingled, volunteers sometimes became confused. Some of the arriving pastor's goods would mistakenly be reloaded and the error not be discovered until the truck was unpacked at the next destination.

Since Gowanda was only about twenty-five miles away by road, father had already made numerous trips with the car, transporting the items most vulnerable to breakage. Father's farming operation still further complicated the task of moving. Most of the farm-related items had to be disposed of. Parting with the farm animals was not easy, for they had become more like family members.

The saying, "You can take the boy off the farm, but you can't take the farm out of the boy," was certainly true with father. Although we were moving to a town of five-thousand, father had found that Lillian Mackmer, one of the members, had a small pasture and barn where he could keep a cow. The best milker of our tiny herd made the move too along with part of the chickens. The rest of the stock was sold - some of it to the new pastor.

I shed no tears as I was freed from servitude to the cream separator, the butter churn, the pump handle, the clothes wringer, and the manure fork. My reluctant forced relationship with them had ended. This realization brought me a sense of freedom and relief!

The parsonage at 156 West Main Street in Gowanda was an old structure with an unusually steep and narrow stairway to the second floor. The stairs made a sharp turn at the top. Upstairs, the roof leaned down to create sloped ceilings which the unwary attempted vainly to raise with their heads. Moving beds and other furniture up these stairs was an impossibility. Father removed an upstairs double-sash window. On a rope, we hoisted the mattresses, bed springs, dressers, and other items up the side of the house and into the bedroom. The truck pulled out of the yard and we were left to settle into our new environment. Father had to prepare his sermon for the next morning, which was Sunday.

On Monday morning I eagerly entered into the life of Gowanda High, a much larger school than Cattaraugus. Both French and Latin were among my favorite courses, partly due to the teachers I was fortunate to have. I forged fast friendships with Bob Rabe, Willis Kirby, and the Cain twins, Bob and Dick, who lived on the road into Zoar Valley.

How I thrilled to the changes in material possessions. The telephone and electrical appliances added amenities with which I was unfamiliar. Mother benefitted the most. She learned to use the Servel gas refrigerator, the Easy twin-tub washing machine, and a gas range. Water, both hot and cold, flowed from the turn of a faucet. A bathroom with tub and the other necessary facilities meant that old Montgomery Ward and Sears catalogs could be discarded instead of saved for recycling in the outhouse. A Grunow cabinet radio brought not only the news, but Major Bowes Amateur Hour, Fibber Magee and Molly, Amos and Andy, and The Shadow.

For me, the greatest of thrills came when father drove into the yard one day with a used 1933 Chrysler. The shiny chrome, sleek lines, and powerful engine accentuated the stodginess of the tired old Chevy he traded in. The new car had two real hot water heaters - one for the back seat and another for the front. Goodbye, soapstones. No more teakettles of hot water or cranking on a cold morning would be necessary to cause this mighty engine to spring to life. This model didn't even have a crank!

* * * * *

Leaving the valley marked the beginning of a long series of major transitions for me. Following high school graduation three years later, attending college at Chesbro (Roberts Wesleyan) became a thrilling reality. This was the school where George Garlock had served as president. After completion of junior college plus one year at Greenville College in Illinois, I was part of the 1943 graduating class at Houghton College.

The valley was left even farther behind as my first real job after graduation began at Bell Aircraft in Buffalo and later Burlington, Vermont. To Burlington I brought my red-headed bride, Betty. After WWII, I spent seven years with a produce firm in Elba, New York. During this period Betty and I became the parents of three children: Bettina, Danny, and Judith. Clearly directed by God, in 1953 we moved this young family to the Kittitas Valley in Washington State. After years of dreaming, I finally found myself in the real West. Here, in this irrigated valley, new vistas opened up in a career as a CPA. The panoply of mountains, lakes, forests, rivers, and ocean exceeded even my wildest imaginings.

In 1960 I felt impelled to respond to an urgent invitation to start a Department of Business Administration at Houghton College in the Genesee River Valley of Western New York. Here Betty began teaching botany and biology. Out of these educational experiences, my glimpses of the world were enlarged to include most of the United States, Canada, and New Zealand.

Standing on a grassy knoll at Cape Rienga at the northern tip of New Zealand, I looked out over the lighthouse, gleaming white in the brilliant sunlight. Just beyond the rugged point, a perceptible line visibly marked the confluence of the water of the Tasman Sea with that of the South Pacific. A signpost announced the distances to faraway points, some of them, like Brooklyn Valley, on the other side of the world. I mused: "How impoverished and narrow my life would have been had I refused to leave Brooklyn Valley!" But, much that I value is a legacy of those years. No matter how fine the setting and experiences, the time comes when one must leave the valley or surrender one's dreams.

Even now, after formal retirement, I still aspire to fresh vistas which stretch far beyond the treasured scenes of the valley of my birth.